PRAISE FOR *OPEN UP, EDUCATION!*: *HOW OPEN WAY LEARNING CAN TRANSFORM SCHOOLS*

"The experiences, lessons, and outcomes shared in *Open Up, Education!* are so much more than just a framework around open way learning. In this day and age, readers, so-called 'reformers,' and rebels often want to find something that works, simply replicate it, and wait for identical results. What I see, and I hope you see, is an intentional focus on the purpose of learning, the outcomes of learner-relevant work, and the value of connecting it to community and collaboration. To that end, I implore readers to celebrate the specific successes from Open Way Learning, but more importantly, focus on the 'how' and the 'why' versus the 'what' and replicate that intentionality for your student, children, and community needs. That's, in my opinion, the secret sauce here. Haigler and Owens have created such a user and reader friendly way to teach adults a lesson (and adults usually don't like to be taught lessons) by showing us what's right in front of us and ready for success. I thank them for teaching me that lesson in *Open Up, Education!*."—Dan Cruce, JD, vice president, Education, Hope Street Group

"I have learned over the years that moving people to action won't take place unless we think behaviors before beliefs. Too many books rely on sophisticated or elegant arguments to be the motivation to act. *Open Up, Education!* describes open source, but it links this with stories of the idea at work. It made it easier for me to envision open source education as a real possibility to help us move beyond our antiquated K–12 learning system."—Mark Sass, teacher, Legacy High School in Denver, CO, and Colorado State Policy Director, Teach Plus

"Haigler and Owens are committed educators who have invested deeply in Tri-County Early College High School, an innovative and progressive institution nestled in the Appalachian Mountains of North Carolina. With their colleagues, they have created a school where students engage in meaningful learning inside their classrooms and with the wide learning beyond. In *Open Up, Education!*, they generously share stories of the practices inside their school and the rich set of research and resources that have inspired them. They understand that great teaching starts not with individual teachers but with a community of educators devoted to building trust, sharing ideas, and working toward continuous improvement."—Justin Reich, EdD, assistant professor, Comparative Media Studies, and director, MIT Teaching Systems Lab, Cambridge, MA

D1521514

"*Open Up, Education!* should give hope to anyone who cares about transforming education. Adam Haigler and Ben Owens have articulated a vision for twenty-first century learning that finally breaks with an industrial-era understanding of how and why we learn. Rather than suggesting new tweaks to an old system, they reimagine how learning can reshape not only individual students but the communities in which they live, learn, and work. Haigler and Owens illustrate how learning centered around collaboration, creativity, and what they call 'intense transparency' is in line with the dynamic shift happening across society more broadly; thus, not only is Open Way Learning a pedagogical model that makes learning personally relevant and intellectually rigorous, but also one that better prepares students for the current information age. *Open Up, Education!* demonstrates what is possible at both micro and macro levels of transformative change, and is a necessary read for educators, administrators, and students who are committed to designing new models of learning."—Aria F. Chernik, JD, PhD, founder and director, Open Source Pedagogy, Research + Innovation, Duke University, Durham, NC

"Haigler and Owens offer a provocative new vision of what education could be. Education leaders, take note of 'The Open Way': teacher-led collaborative teams can unlock innovation, student success, and teacher satisfaction like you've never seen."—Bryan C. Hassel, PhD, copresident, Public Impact & The Opportunity Culture Initiative

"*Open Up, Education!* makes a great case for why Open Way Learning is needed in education."—Stephanie (Abraham) Hirsh, PhD, executive director, Learning Forward

"The application of open source philosophies and practices in education that is described in *Open Up, Education!* is both brilliant and inspirational. The structure of the open source way applied to learning is obvious, as the book outlines the path to building the learning equivalent to Red Hat, while not ignoring the challenges that exist in taking that journey. At Red Hat, I've lived a constantly evolving process built on collaboration, remix, transparency, and community. I have always believed that these core open source tenets can and should be applied to the way that students learn, and this work provides a vital next step: the plan to actually do it. Through innovation and real world experience, students can be prepared to not just survive but thrive. The authors of this book see that and embrace it! *Open Up, Education!* serves as a reminder that the open source way ethos is indeed changing the world!"—Tom Callaway, University Outreach and Fedora Special Projects, Red Hat, Inc.

"High praise for *Open, Up, Education!* Taking inspiration from intellectual innovators around the world and under our noses, Haigler and Owens do a masterful job of explaining how we can—and why we must—move from supporting students as passive consumers to active creators of their own education experience."—Rachel Belin, director, Prichard Committee Student Voice Team, Lexington, KY

"This work is tremendously important. The world is rapidly changing around us and we need new and better stories to tell about how we're going to address the wicked problems we're facing. Haigler and Owens have done a masterful job demonstrating how we can reframe what learning means in the world today. Previously, education systems tried to address student learning in a closed system: very isolated, very insular, and irrespective of *who* was in the room. They have crafted a masterful blueprint that will challenge and inspire you to think about how to open up learning for *everyone,* including teachers, parents, and community members. Education desperately needs to be open and expansive, pushing against the artificial walls and boundaries we have constructed over the years. Haigler and Owens will show you how."—Greg Garner, research associate, The William and Ida Friday Institute for Educational Innovation

"It's the twenty-first century; of course, schools should open up! But how can teachers and academic leaders leverage open source principles as a guide for progressive education? Haigler and Owens skillfully connect the open source model with creative classroom practices to produce a compelling framework for the future of schools. Filled with clear examples and ideas, *Open Up, Education!* challenges ineffective classroom practices and reframes teaching and learning for an increasingly complex, collaborative, and interconnected world."—Charlie Reisinger, technology director, Penn Manor School District, Lancaster, PA, and author, *The Open Schoolhouse*

"If our organizations are to thrive and succeed in a global economy, our education system needs to prepare our students for the twenty-first and twenty-second centuries. As Haigler and Owens hypothesize, the path to sustainable organizational success requires a culture of collaboration, the free exchange of knowledge, and an innovation ethos. If this is true for business, why would we want to structure education in a rigid, formulaic way based on a 150-year-old model? Shouldn't our educational system foster these same ideals? The Open Way Learning framework provides educators—and businesses—a roadmap on how to drive change in education to facilitate dramatic long-term economic and social impact."—Jason H. Parker, marketing communications assistant, Davidson Day School, Davidson, NC, and TechStars Startup Weekend Global Facilitator

"*Open Up, Education!* is an excellent read for any educator interested in reimagining school and creating new ways for students to learn and grow. Haigler and Owens make a compelling case that teachers are better working together than siloed into closed doored classrooms. The power of opening up is evident throughout the book and inspires all educators to lift their voices and share their work. This is a better way for students and teachers."—Amy Junge, director, Teacher-Powered Schools, Education Evolving

"It is so refreshing to have educators write books from experience. Not as a 'do these steps to be successful' but as a 'here is what worked for us, now adapt it to your situation.' *Open Up, Education!* does exactly that."—Carla Jones, J. W. Cook Elementary School, Chicago, IL

"*Open Up, Education!* does a great job of connecting very specific education-related ideas and principles to more broad ideals we should be considering in our lives and the world."—Aaron Kaswell, Blended Mathematics & STEAM teacher, MS88, New York City Department of Education, Brooklyn, NY

"I think Haigler and Owens have done some really important work for educators. We have traditionally worked in an isolated field, leaving many of us to feel as though we are practicing on an island. As a result, our successes and failures often go unnoticed. We don't help others learn from them or replicate them. It is time for education to grow and for us to open up about our practice so that we can all move forward for student learning."—Jason Boll, English teacher, Pittsburgh Perry High School, Pittsburgh, PA

"*Open Up, Education!* arrives at a pivotal moment in America's educational journey. With the need to reimagine school around community connectedness and personalized experiences, Adam Haigler and Ben Owens provide a guided path forward with Open Way Learning. This book gives educators and community leaders the tools to create relevant learning experiences grounded in collaboration, innovation, and open access to knowledge. Open Way Learning pivots education to prepare all students for the twenty-first-century gig economy."—Nathan Strenge, head of math department, The International School of Minnesota, Eden Prairie, MN

"Teaching and learning is a delicate science. We need books like this and colleagues like Haigler and Owens to help us continue the work of transforming schools."—Meg Turner, EdM, principal, Charles D. Owen High School, Asheville, NC

"When Ben Owens gave up his very successful engineering career in industry to become a teacher of math and physics, I was surprised and somewhat saddened to lose a cherished collaborator, confidante, and colleague. After reading *Open Up, Education!*, I understand. Owens has combined learnings from his tremendously successful careers in industry and education to develop a practical approach to Open Way Learning that educators can apply to their own practice—complete with checklists!"—Jay Wirsig, global engineering manager, DuPont, and member and board of directors, Providence Care, Ontario, Canada

"The brilliance of Haigler and Owens's work is that is so applicable to much of the work driving education across the nation. *Open Up, Education!* is written in language that educators at any stage of their career can understand and implement in their instructional practice. Input from teacher leaders and educational experts help to frame the work in a way that is easily applied to professional roles from classroom practitioners to district leaders. I highly recommend it!"—MeMe Ratliff, Teacher Engagement Resource teacher, Jefferson County Public Schools, Louisville, KY, and cofounder, JCPSForward

"*Open Up, Education!* is essential reading for any educator who is interested in seeing examples of how educators are opening up their minds—and the minds of their students—within this country and the world. The real world, applicable connections of teachers is enough to inspire you to look beyond the curriculum you know."—Orly Mondell, resource teacher, Office of Blended Learning; freshmen coordinator; and social studies teacher, Pikesville High School, Baltimore County Public Schools, MD

"Every teacher and school leader should read this book! *Open Up, Education!* gives them the resources, research, and steps to change schools to meet students where they are and give them what they need. I love this book and am very excited to share its ideas with my colleagues and district leaders."— Andrea Quintana, Zuni Elementary instructional coach, Albuquerque, NM

"*Open Up, Education!* brings to light the critical relationship between organizational culture and organizational success at a time where schools and districts are adapting to the changing nature of the educational landscape. What Haigler and Owens highlight is the need to reimagine the way that school cultures operate in an age where what happens within the wall of a schoolhouse does not effectively prepare students for the world beyond those walls. Throughout the text, examples are provided and scrutinized for their merits by the authors and a clear approach to open education is provided. What this work accomplishes is not in creating a singular approach or path to organizational success but in causing the reader to pause and reflect on how their organization does or does not prepare students for positive life outcomes. The authors challenge our current perceptions about teaching and learning and give us the opportunity to reflect on both our current state and where we need to go."—Gregory Mullenholz, principal, Ashburton Elementary School, Montgomery County, MD, and 2011 US Department of Education Washington Teaching Fellow

"State legislators and governmental educational leaders need to read this book! They have had a heavy hand in educational policy and have tended to use the stick in the form of high-stakes testing. This book is full of hope, philosophy, and specifics for passionate educators to move forward. Before retiring I was an active participant in research-based reform at a small rural middle school. It was exciting to apply many of the concepts and practices described by Haigler and Owens, but it fell apart when our supportive principal left. I do think that there are many islands of effective innovation in the teaching profession but it needs to be system-wide."—Connie Kennedy, PhD, middle school counselor (ret.), Union City, MI

"This is the perfect read for any teacher leader or administrator looking to pull their school out of the dark ages and into now! I'm so excited for my colleagues to read this so we can get started opening up education . . . together."—Anna E. Baldwin, EdD, 2014 Montana Teacher of the Year and 2016–2017 US Department of Education Teaching Ambassador Fellow

"*Open Up Education!* is committed to the idea that kids learn better by doing interesting and authentic activities, that test scores are only a small part of the goal of a school, and that the purpose of education is to build skills and processes that students can use for the rest of their lives. It is an incredible resource for educators who want to change their practice, their classrooms, and their schools."—Jeremy Thompson, assistant principal, Mountain Island Charter School, Mt. Holly, NC

Open Up, Education!

Open Up, Education!

How Open Way Learning Can Transform Schools

Adam Haigler
Ben Owens

ROWMAN & LITTLEFIELD
Lanham • Boulder • New York • London

Published by Rowman & Littlefield
An imprint of The Rowman & Littlefield Publishing Group, Inc.
4501 Forbes Boulevard, Suite 200, Lanham, Maryland 20706
www.rowman.com

6 Tinworth Street, London SE11 5AL

British Library Cataloguing in Publication Information Available

Library of Congress Cataloging-in-Publication Data

Names: Haigler, Adam, 1984– author. | Owens, Ben, 1964– author.
Title: Open up, education! : how open way learning can transform schools / Adam Haigler, Ben Owens.
Description: Lanham : Rowman & Littlefield, [2018] | Includes bibliographical references.
Identifiers: LCCN 2018029427 | ISBN 9781475841992 (cloth : alk. paper) | ISBN 9781475842005 (pbk. : alk. paper)
Subjects: LCSH: Group work in education—Software. | Distance education—Computer-assisted instruction. | School improvement programs. | Open source software.
Classification: LCC LB1032 .H344c2018 | DDC 371.39/5—dc23
LC record available at https://lccn.loc.gov/2018029427

∞™ The paper used in this publication meets the minimum requirements of American National Standard for Information Sciences—Permanence of Paper for Printed Library Materials, ANSI/NISO Z39.48-1992.

Printed in the United States of America

Contents

Foreword

Times have changed. Ten years ago, when I started describing my teaching methods as Open Source Learning, the idea of allowing students to use the Internet in class to connect with people and publicly curate their work was new. Like most anything new in education, it was also regarded as risky; journalists who interviewed me asked me if I was afraid of losing my job.

Today the virtual world sometimes feels safer for students than the real one. The week before I wrote this foreword, a nineteen-year-old gunman opened fire with an assault rifle in a Florida high school and killed seventeen students, leading to an American debate about gun control that featured far-fetched suggestions such as arming teachers.

Exploring these issues in the wake of tragedy is, of course, vital for our society. But almost no one in the national media is talking about how events like this affect student learning or the ways young people see themselves and their places in our society. The murders in Florida brought the issue of school safety into tragically clear focus. They also highlighted the many political, cultural, and economic forces that threaten the viability of public education. Public education needs us.

In this book, you'll read how Adam and Ben have used Open Source Learning practices to help students thrive. Understanding the challenges and opportunities in today's schools will enable you to take the greatest advantage of the experiences and strategies they describe. We can begin by considering the purpose and function for school in the information age.

Human beings beat other species to the top of the food chain for two reasons: first, we're better at learning, and, second, we're better at telling stories about what we've learned. These gifts enable large numbers of us to connect, cooperate, and evolve through the abstract ideas that we create. You can go anywhere in the world, and no matter what language you speak, you can instantly recognize local rituals and share a sense of belonging and identification with strangers through ideas and stories about ideas: a country, a religion, a sports team, a corporate brand, or a way of life.

Because learning and telling stories are the defining characteristic of our species, it makes sense that learning feels so . . . *good*! Solving a problem or mastering a skill is a welcome challenge. As children we crave these experiences; we ask dozens of questions a day, and our growing brains forge new neuronal connections and schema so we can categorize and store all that new information. Whee!

Learning is good and we know it in our bones—that's thousands of years of evolution talking. We love the idea and the experience of learning, and we should be careful not to confuse learning with schooling. As one of my students wrote, "Students love learning, but hate to be taught." We have all the raw ingredients for inspired, enthusiastic learning. We love doing things so much that we push ourselves past our comfort zones. We make mistakes and we don't give up. We keep practicing. Our determined resilience doesn't come from the promise of reward or the threat of punishment, or even from an internal sense of discipline—it's the result of a drive as strong as thirst.

As much as we love to learn, our system of education is a big problem. Traditional approaches to education impede learning by forcing us to obey, conform, and work in isolation. Over time, our desire shifts from understanding and mastery to seeking rewards and avoiding punishment. The reasons are all too familiar: we want to learn about subjects that aren't taught in school, we learn best by doing and collaborating with others, we suffer through boring "one-too-many" lectures under strict time constraints, we feel vulnerable when teachers and students crush our natural passions and curiosities. Eventually we learn not to resist as teachers demand specific behaviors. We learn how to avoid the discomfort of vulnerability. We give up on asking questions, challenging assumptions, and taking other sorts of constructive risks that lead to accelerated learning and becoming our best selves.

It doesn't have to be this way.

As Adam and Ben demonstrate in this book, we can use Open Source Learning principles and the tools of our age to create wonderful opportunities for the members of learning communities to be their best selves. When I left teaching positions at the University of California, Los Angeles, and a management consulting practice to teach high school in 2004, I started by using online technology to save paper, to enliven the curriculum, and to support students who weren't able to attend class. I quickly realized that the Internet was developing a culture all its own and that it was bigger and, in many ways, better than what students could get in school.

But school is a closed system. Students sit in a room where nonstudents are not allowed without a special pass. Students are told what to do and how to do it, and they are given an assignment to demonstrate their understanding. They write on a piece of paper, then the teacher scribbles a grade on it and returns it. Students stuff it in their binders or crumple it in the bottom of their backpacks. All that work and only two people see it. In fact, apart from the students' transcripts, which are protected by privacy laws, almost all school-work is a secret that is quickly lost. In the endless discussion of the disconnect between formal education and what we become for the rest of our lives, it is a constant irony that most schooling involves isolated study while personal lives and careers demand teamwork. And the only place we compartmental-ize life into subject-by-subject instruction is in the K–12 experience.

Closed learning systems reinforce traditional roles: active teacher and passive students. I wanted to create learning environments where everyone starts from a place of understanding and agreement and then customizes the experience to answer their own big questions and create personalized, inter-disciplinary learning journeys. That is how Open Source Learning began to emerge. I began cultivating opportunities to create virtual learning communi-ties of interest and critique. Open systems exchange components and energy and ideas with the surrounding world. I wanted to bring the world to my students and my students to the world, and open systems gave me a structural way to think about what I was trying to accomplish. Open-source models of collaboration and software development extended my thinking.

In Open Source Learning, each student refines the curriculum to meet her individual needs and interests. Every big question is an interdisciplinary one: a cup of tea is not just a cup of tea—it is an invitation to explore botany, ce-ramics, the history of colonialism, and the invisible forces that hold the cup to the table.

With this interdisciplinary approach, academic subjects become relevant, essential building blocks of understanding. Open-source learners realize that physics reveals the secrets of skateboarding and that biology and probability demystify dating; as a result, their world becomes magical and motivating. The outcome of a student's work becomes an online, multimedia portfolio that creates immediate value for the learner and the reader alike. These op-portunities transform a student's ability to learn and—perhaps even more important—to collaborate. Every day I see this in students who team with peers and mentors online.

I have worked with Open Source Learning networks on several continents that involve thousands of learners and educators, and I have seen countless beautiful moments of support, concern, and genuine empathy. It's no longer enough for our education system to churn out graduates. We have become interdependent in ways we don't yet fully understand, and we need each other. Open Source Learning helps students become empowered, well-rounded human beings who create value, support interdependence, and give us all hope.

Learning and collaboration happen wherever we're open to it. On January 22, 2016, I woke up before dawn in New York City. I checked the weather and realized I would have to move quickly; a massive blizzard was approaching, and I needed to find a flight home before the airports closed. But everything was booked. I worked the phone and the Internet, and lucked into the last seat on the last flight out of Philadelphia.

I hustled to Penn Station, ran for the train, collapsed into a seat, and breathed a sigh of relief, hoping I would get to the plane and it would get off the ground before the airport shut down. That's when I opened my email and met Adam: "Hi Dr. Preston, I am a teacher in rural western North Carolina at a high school that is currently revitalizing its model. . . ." Over the last two years it has been my great privilege to get to know Adam and Ben, and to watch as they have used Open Source Learning principles to expand and enrich their learning community. I am inspired by their work, and I think you will be, too.

The future is complicated and uncertain, and it is also full of opportunity. We will need to learn our way through it and adapt our system of education to align with what we do best as our culture and technology continue to evolve. Reading this book is a wonderful next step.

David Preston, PhD

Acknowledgments

The outpouring of support as we developed the ideas for this book was beyond anything we ever expected. So many people offered advice, ideas, and encouragement that to try listing each one would inevitably mean we would be leaving people out. We are eternally grateful to all the people we interacted with as we took a crazy idea and built it into something worth sharing with people all over the world. The positive feedback from educators, especially those on the cutting edge of this new open movement, has been nothing short of incredible and provided the fuel we needed when we were questioning our ability to pull off the daunting task of writing a book while still being fully committed to our day jobs as teachers.

We are especially grateful for the support of David Preston and David Price, who generously gave us their perspectives and insights on this movement. It was a true test of "openness" and trust for them to collaborate with us so deeply. Their unyielding excitement and encouragement validated our direction and expanded our passion for this work. Taking the time to carefully read our manuscript and provide feedback, then visiting us and our school after a few short interactions, were incredibly meaningful gestures. We can't thank the David P.'s enough for their support!

Lauri Moffett, Rae Nelson, Karl Haigler, and Gwen Owens each provided valuable editorial work that streamlined some of our obtuse language. Lauri's edits showed a remarkable attention to detail that has made this book more readable and grammatically correct! Karl and Rae gave excellent suggestions and moral support that kept us moving and improving the manuscript at every stage. Gwen was a constant source of support and encouragement who reminded us to simplify our message to increase its potency.

A special acknowledgment is in order for our colleagues and students at Tri-County Early College, who inspire us daily and provide a venue to develop and refine many of the ideas presented in this book! We also will be forever indebted to our spouses, Allison and Hygie, who have offered their patience and moral support for this adventure. The many late nights and weekends we invested were facilitated by their unwavering encouragement. This book would have been impossible without you!

What Is Open Way Learning?

In open source, we feel strongly that to really do something well, you have to get a lot of people involved.—Linus Torvalds, creator of the Linux kernel

THE HOMETOWN HERITAGE PROJECT

The Hometown Heritage project was ideal for Tri-County Early College. The project was based on the Foxfire project from Rabun County, Georgia, about an hour away. During the 1970s, students at Rabun Gap Nacoochee School documented the skills and oral histories of local people in the area and compiled them into magazines. These stories eventually became the basis for a popular book series. Modeling a project around Foxfire seemed a perfect way to engage our high school with our community, deepen their learning of curricular content, and teach them skills they could use for a lifetime. It also meant taking a risk.

To elevate the public nature of the project, we reached out to the John C. Campbell Folk School, a century-old bastion of Appalachian tradition only a couple of miles from our school, to see how we might take advantage of their facilities and resident artists and experts. The executive director of the Folk School was eager to work with us and offered to support us in any way possible. After some initial meetings, our students were granted permission to present a living history museum at the Folk School as their final exhibition.

The kickoff of the project had gone swimmingly well, and students had organized their own groups around far-ranging interests that included hide tanning, soap making, herbal medicine, cabin building, and traditional clogging.

Each group recruited mentors who would help them learn their skill of choice and conducted oral history interviews with locals to be featured in their group's e-book chapter. They also worked with their teachers to demonstrate how they were integrating curricular knowledge into their project presentations.

One group even embarked on the ambitious goal of relocating a historic cabin from a staff member's property to the Folk School, where it could be a museum exhibit. We were quite skeptical, given that the group attracted a large number of freshmen boys renowned for their "squirreliness." Fortunately, two juniors signed onto the team and showed tremendous leadership. One of the juniors, Jack, was intent on proving all the doubters, including his father, wrong.

As the final exhibition loomed, anxiety mounted. The school's public relations class had created a website, social media campaign, logo, flyers, press release, and eight-page exhibition program while coordinating the logistics of the event with the Folk School. The stakes felt higher after the Facebook event was reposted to the Folk School's more than thirty thousand followers, resulting in over one hundred community members planning to attend!

The day of the event finally arrived, and the normal exhibition-day butterflies were now piranhas! However, as students set up and practiced at their tables, the magic gradually surfaced. The centerpiece of the exhibition was the cabin, which the eight students miraculously constructed after arduous weekends of hauling, notching, and roofing. It was surrounded by students demonstrating blacksmithing, making Civil War drum calls, and doling out samples of smoked meat. Across the trail students showcased basketry, canning, and Appalachian foodways, which meant tantalizing smells wafting through the air.

Over three hundred guests attended the most impressive exhibition our school had ever produced. The students were delighted by the throngs of interested onlookers, while the visitors were beyond captivated with the depth of understanding and passion our students exemplified. The cabin group had a perpetual crowd that clamored to hear them play traditional Appalachian songs and enthusiastically discuss their connections to math, science, history, and English.

When Adam ran into Jack on the way down a trail to another part of the exhibition, he stopped him, looked him in the eye, and said, "I'm so proud of you." He teared up and replied, "Thanks, man. You don't know how much that means to me." Adam could tell by the stunned look on the face of Jack's father, who hung out around the cabin the whole night, that he was proud too.

The next week, the local paper gave the project an entire page of colorful coverage. The community was abuzz with excitement as the video showing the exhibition got over seven thousand views on Facebook.[1] That risk of "opening up" the work of our school on its biggest stage was rewarded with a groundswell of community support and profound student learning experiences.

Figure 1.1. A student talks with a community member attending the exhibition about the cabin his group constructed.
Photo by Tipper Pressley.

   This true story perfectly illustrates the inherent potency of a different way to approach teaching and learning: an *innovative* approach where students clearly see the relevance of their work by sharing it in the public domain, virtually and in person, *collaborate* to share ideas, and synergize their work to make their own classrooms and schools more engaging and impactful for students. It is a model where the *free sharing* of projects via a website or social media invites the larger community to contribute to student learning and maybe even reuse the project in their own schools. We call this framework Open Way Learning. Curious? Read on.

OPEN OR CLOSED?

Do you benefit from a population that's smarter, faster, and more connected than it used to be?
Do you prefer transparency?
Either you're riding the tide or pushing against it.
Are you hoping that those you serve become more informed or less informed?
Are you working to give people more autonomy or less?

Do you want them to work to seek the truth, or to be clouded in disbelief
    and confusion?
Is it better if they're connected to one another or disconnected?
More confidence or more fear?
Outspoken in the face of injustice or silent?
More independent or less?
Difficult to control or easier? More science or more obedience?
It's pretty clear that there are forces on both sides, individuals and orga-
    nizations that are working for open and those that seek to keep things
    closed instead.
Take a side.

This pithy set of questions frames the premise of this book and was posed in a 2017 blog by Seth Godin, the bestselling author and former dot-com business executive.[2] The premise is that by adopting what we are calling an Open Way mindset, educators have the perfect opportunity to accelerate the pace of innovative thinking and learning that can finally break away from a model of industrialized education that has dominated our schools for far too long.

Forward-thinking people and organizations across the globe are embracing such a model through engaged collective action, intense transparency, and creative thought to make our legacy systems of government, corporations, and even militaries that are more responsive to the needs of the communities they serve. This dynamic shift is happening throughout society, where openness is becoming the expected norm and not the exception. Organizations unwilling to respond to this wave of openness are destined to march down a slow path to irrelevance. We believe that is, to a large extent, also the case in education if something is not done to alter the course. Now.

In all likelihood, you have a device within arm's length that has more computing power than the rocket that took men to the moon, you are more connected with people across the planet than all your ancestors combined, and you probably know children who can write code at an age when you were just learning to write your name. Why is it that technology evolves so much faster than our education systems? Why is the smartphone in your pocket going to be obsolete in three years while certain classroom designs—with desks facing a lecturing teacher—have endured for over a century? Is it because this educational model is so effective that we would be foolish to abandon it? Probably not. Most importantly, what are the impacts of education's stasis in a rapidly changing global economy and environment?

This book is an attempt to answer questions such as these and, in doing so, to offer a new way of thinking—an open approach to how we teach and learn with our children.

THE OPEN-SOURCE MINDSET

The questions posed above foreshadow the explorations we will take throughout this book, but don't let the name "open source" fool you. This book is not about fixing education with technology, computing, or big data. This book is about a mindset. A culture. A pedagogy. This philosophy has its roots in the coding world of software development, but it is a cultural movement that reaches far beyond programming. To understand this movement, and the profound implications it has on the education ecosystem, we need to provide some background that dips into the realm of software development. This diversion into the open-source coding world will set the stage for what unfolds in the rest of the book.

Whether you realize it or not, open-source software is ubiquitous in today's world. Here's how it works. One programmer creates a so-called source code that does something useful. Then she or he publishes this code to a community of other programmers, who take the source code and remix it. They may use it to design a new program, debug glitches, or make small adaptations that make it work for their specific application, creating a source code that may be completely different from what was first published. This system is highly dependent on what's called a crowdsourced review: through iteration and constant tinkering, the software becomes more stable and more reliable—and often becomes a much cheaper alternative to proprietary software developed by corporations such as Microsoft and Apple.

A classic example is Linux, an open-source operating system that was created in 1991 by Linus Torvalds. It has become the backbone of almost every technology we use, including Android phones, car computers, web servers, and other software, as well as applications used everywhere from the military to Wall Street. Torvalds, a Finnish software engineering student at the time, is said to have begun the open-source revolution when he developed the Linux operating system. After posting his initial development to a mailing list, coders from across the world began sharing ideas to make the original code better. Before too long, this user-led effort became one of the biggest collaborative projects in history: open-source software.

The open-source approach enlists a virtual army of coders who are not bound to the centralized institutional restrictions of companies or countries. Anyone anywhere who can add value to the code can do so. These decentralized coders work in parallel to manage themselves and, in so doing, iterate faster than their less numerous counterparts in private organizations.

More eyes on the code—this is where the term "code talks" comes from—results in continuous improvement and a much more rapid and incremental release schedule than that of proprietary software.[3] In fact,

Linux-based systems are famous for being much less prone to attacks from malware than privately held software, because such attacks are quickly identified and thwarted by the community of users, like white blood cells attacking a virus.[4]

Entire products and companies also operate with an open-source approach. One example is Red Hat, a publicly traded software company based in North Carolina whose mission is to create customized, open-source software and networking solutions for their customers. Although Red Hat may not be a "household name," their competency has led 90 percent of Fortune 500 companies to hire them. Their unique business model is eloquently described by their motto: "The code is free, we add the value."[5]

Open source is not just restricted to companies like Red Hat. Indeed, some of the most cutting-edge technology companies have embraced the practice of sharing their source code precisely because they see the advantages of rapid, crowdsourced innovation. Microsoft, Amazon, Tesla, Hewlett Packard, Adobe, Google, and Samsung have all strategically released source code in some fashion in the last twenty years and have obviously remained powerhouses in the technology market.[6]

So why would organizations, especially privately held corporations that must answer to shareholders, be willing to share information, even with so-called competitors? When we asked Allen Blue, the cofounder of LinkedIn, he highlighted the open sharing inherent in the culture of Silicon Valley: "[Silicon Valley has] an open, crowdsourced environment where everyone from tech giants to new start-ups benefits from the same corpus of experience. In fact, I can't even remember a time when people thought that it was unique to collaborate! Sure, you will have takers and freeloaders, but the low cost of sharing and the benefit of sharing makes it worth it." Open-source communities recognize that the core tenet of the open-source model is the power of the crowd rather than any one individual or small group of "experts." Consider crowd-crafting and how it intersects with the growing popularity of citizen science, for example.

In crowd-crafted projects, professional scientists collaborate with amateurs in an online community. These citizen science projects encompass everything from the environment and astronomy to the human genome. The discovery of the Higgs boson, a previously unknown elementary particle, is one such example. Physicists from around the world were tapped to probe the vast amount of data from the Large Hadron Collider experiments, which were designed to reveal new subatomic particles by colliding two high-energy particle beams that travel nearly the speed of light. This same open-source approach has now become an accepted best practice for employing the expertise of many for the advancement of scientific research.[7]

THE OPEN SOURCE WAY

With this background, we can begin to glimpse the game-changing characteristics of the open-source approach and its potential to create positive disruption in areas well beyond software development. Coders who pioneered the open-source movement generally subscribe to certain principles, called the "Open Source Way," that are applicable to nonsoftware enterprises. This philosophy not only encourages but demands open exchange, collaborative participation, rapid prototyping, meritocracy, and community-oriented development.[8] It embraces the "code talks" to drive innovation through intense collaboration and open sharing. But, could these tenets be fruitfully applied outside of software development?

Let us briefly return to Red Hat to see how an open-source culture that had its nexus in software can have a transformative impact well beyond coding. An open organization innovates internally while also finding and leveraging expertise with stakeholders outside.

In his recent book *The Open Organization*, Red Hat CEO Jim Whitehurst focuses his attention on the characteristics of what he calls the "Open Source Way," illustrating how the open-source ethos is applied to an organization so it can become more nimble and responsive to the needs of its stakeholders. Two essential characteristics he identifies are passion and engagement throughout the organization. Without these, the energy to run an open organization won't exist.

Like good citizenship, participating in a community like this requires being informed, communicative, and proactive. Each of these takes effort, which if not managed well can drain individual and collective energy. When done well, as author Daniel Pink emphasizes in his bestseller *Drive: The Surprising Truth about What Motivates Us*, characteristics of the Open Source Way can lead to a passion for one's work based on purpose, autonomy, and mastery.

As Pink stated, "The secret to high performance and satisfaction . . . is the deeply human need to direct our own lives, to learn and create new things, and to do better by ourselves and our world." In the case of Red Hat, this emphasis creates a culture with a default to openness, where rapid innovation is the norm. Rather than money or title, the passion for one's work inspires, motivates, and rewards people to perform at the highest level. The way Whitehurst describes it, "purpose is the baseline, but when you add passion, it's like adding gasoline on the fire."

In open organizations, natural leaders are chosen by the community based on the merit of their ideas, not by title or credentials. The coordination of work, collaboration, and organizational structures for each task flows organically from these informal leaders based on mutual respect rather than top-down mandates. The functionality of an open organization also depends on transparent, candid dialogue.

Whitehurst mentions that everyone at Red Hat thinks it is their "God-given right to complain." Though destructive complaints are toxic, constructive criticism is fundamental to the Open Source Way because of its emphasis on product and process improvement. Accepting and encouraging this culture is an early and essential part of opening an organization. Kim Scott, former executive at Google and Apple, calls this "radical candor" in her book *Radical Candor: Be a Kickass Boss without Losing Your Humanity.*

Finally, inclusive decision-making is crucial. Many companies and schools feign interest in employee feedback with the proverbial "suggestion box" that never gets reviewed. However, an authentic open organization will establish a deep level of trust throughout the organization and then solicit feedback and empower frontline employees to be primary decision makers. Though the front end of this process is more time consuming, Whitehurst notes that the notorious buy-in phase is much easier because employees own the decision and don't need to be coerced into compliance.

THE OPEN WAY IN EDUCATION

> Open Education seeks to scale educational opportunities by taking advantage of the power of the Internet, allowing rapid and essentially free dissemination, and enabling people around the world to access knowledge, connect and collaborate. Open is key; open allows not just access, but the ability to modify and use materials, information and networks so education can be personalized to individual users or woven together in new ways for large and diverse audiences.—The Open Education Consortium

What has been presented to this point should provide the reader with a clearer picture of the Open Way. Ideally, by describing its foundations the reader will be better able to recognize what is truly open and where the term "open" has fallen victim to the same buzzword fate as so many other terms in education.

The idea for this book emerged from our school's experimentation with the concept of Open Source Learning, first pioneered by David Preston in high school classes in California. Preston defines Open Source Learning as "an educational practice that allows students to use the internet, social media, and interdisciplinary inquiry to create and manage their own learning experiences that can be shared online with everyone."

Preston had students write blogs instead of term papers, then had them communicate directly with authors and peers regarding the books they were reading and writing about. We "remixed" Preston's methods to launch a unique version of Open Source Learning across our entire school, a version heavily infused with project-based learning and competency-based education.

As we discussed the idea of writing the book, we realized that our unique version of school-wide Open Source Learning coupled with the notion of applying the Open Way more broadly to the entire education system required a different term. Thus, Open Way Learning (OWL) was born. Open Source Learning is one practice that still fits under the umbrella of Open Way Learning, but the latter implies a scope beyond the classroom that can transform entire educational systems, networks, and districts.

Can the Open Way—which is based on passion, engagement, meritocracy, candid dialogue, and inclusive decision-making—work in an education system that is notoriously driven by top-down decisions, heavy with controlling bureaucracy, obsessed with standardization, and disposed to attitudes that reward isolation and hoarding? Definitely.

OPEN SOURCE LEARNING

David Preston, a PhD management consultant turned high school teacher, was the first practitioner of Open Source Learning (he actually coined the term back in 2012). He highlights his visionary and pioneering work in a 2013 TEDx talk at the University of California, Los Angeles.[1] David's work as a lecturer at UCLA and at Santa Maria Joint Union High School District in California helped inform Ben and Adam's own efforts to apply the Open Source Learning framework to Tri-County Early College as part of the school's application for the XQ Super School competition.

David's efforts also provide a case study in how to apply the OWL characteristics to create a powerful student learning environment that disrupts the traditional classroom model. First, he facilitated a set of student interviews with authors and then had the students follow up with a series of collaborative blogs and a thriving web presence. This allowed his students to deepen their knowledge of English and writing. Moreover, raising the stakes and making their work public provided them with real-world relevance and connections that no traditional classroom experience could touch.

Preston's primary focus was within in his own classroom, but it exemplifies how even a single teacher can take advantage of collaboration, free sharing of knowledge, and innovation to create a thriving and relevant learning environment for students. In his words: "We educators come to things from our own perspectives. So even the old school model can be open source if you are willing to create a learning community that goes beyond the school walls to find outside experts and then present the student work in a way that has a massive public audience."

1. "Open Source Learning: David Preston at TEDxUCLA," YouTube video, 10:36, filmed March 22, 2013, posted by TEDx Talks, March 22, 2013, https://www.youtube.com/watch?v=mp0-QQQgv7s.

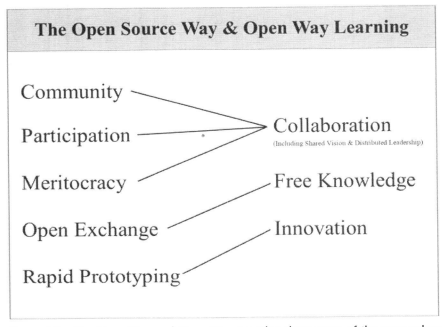

Figure 1.2.   The Open Way and Open Way Learning share many of the same values and principles.

The whole ideal on which free, public education is based—one where every child has an equal shot and where ability defines one's value—is perfectly aligned with the core values of an open-source approach. Unfortunately, this ideal gets diluted by rules and procedures that emphasize control, conformity, and the way it has always been done. Throughout this book, we intend to highlight how each characteristic of the Open Way can be adapted and emphasized to work in the educational ecosystem and to return us to this original vision of providing a free, high-quality education for all children.

To simplify the Open Way and adapt it for education, we have consolidated and reframed some of its principles. Figure 1.2 shows how the Open Source Way connects to Open Way Learning's three main components: collaboration, free knowledge, and innovation.

THE OWL SOURCE CODE

Any book about the Open Way in education would be incomplete without acknowledging the power of open technology. Nevertheless, this book is less about open education resources (OER) and more about how to employ an Open Way mindset to foster critically needed collaboration, sharing of ideas and resources, and innovation between students and education professionals. As such, we turn now to the less known but in our view equally important cultural aspects of Open Way Learning. By using the Open Way, our schools can better develop the dispositions, attributes, and skills our children need to thrive in a rapidly changing world.

Throughout the book we highlight examples from significant pioneers who either developed or are currently championing an Open Way approach in education. We will loosely organize these sources into three areas: student learning, teacher learning, and school governance.

We will present some of the "source code" most closely linked to what we espouse in this book, providing the foundation on which we will build our

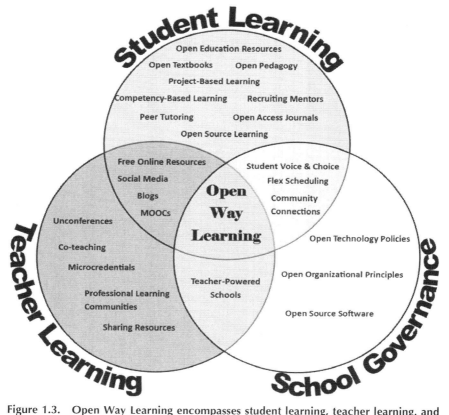

Figure 1.3. Open Way Learning encompasses student learning, teacher learning, and school governance.

case for structural change within education. However, the samples we have included throughout the book do not represent every organization, individual, and event within the Open Way Learning community.

Given the decentralized nature of Open Way Learning, as well as its reach into technology, workforce development, and higher education (areas that are for the most part beyond the scope of this book), any attempt to provide a comprehensive description will inevitably be incomplete. The point of our approach is to shine a light on resources, people, and programs that are foundational to Open Way Learning so the reader can see that this movement is indeed well underway, albeit in varying degrees, in locations across the world.

Another seminal resource on the open education movement, *Open: The Philosophy and Practices that are Revolutionizing Education and Science*, offers one such example. William Huitt and David Monetti's chapter, "Openness and the Transformation of Education and Schooling," addresses the urgent cultural shift as openness becomes the expected norm and not the exception. This expectation, especially of the current generation, is focused on ideals of transparency, inclusivity, collaboration, agility, adaptability, and community. Huitt and Monetti elegantly illustrate the contrast between open education and traditional education in table 1.1, and the astute reader will immediately recognize that the open education column is also deeply rooted in the characteristics of the Open Way.

Table 1.1.   Traditional vs. Open Educational Approaches

	Traditional	*Open*
Transparency	Opaque or hidden data and decision-making processes	Transparent data and decision-making processes
Purpose	Socializing for factory work	Socializing for global democracy
Focus	Curriculum-centered	Person-centered
Desired outcomes	Cognitive	Holistic
Assessment	Discrete cognitive knowledge	Authentic, holistic profile
Teaching processes	Standardized, directed learning	Varied, as appropriate, with more self-regulated learning
Learning tasks	Curriculum-directed	Problem- and project-based
Resources	Private enterprise controlled	Free or inexpensive
Work environment	Compartmentalized	Connected
Organizational structure	Centralized	Decentralized

This table shows the differences between traditional and open educational approaches. Source: William Huitt and David Monetti, "Openness and the Transformation of Education and Schooling," in *Open: The Philosophy and Practices That Are Revolutionizing Education and Science*, ed. Rajiv Jhangiani and Robert Biswas-Diener, 43–65 (London: Ubiquity, 2017).

Another acknowledged leader in open education who must be mentioned at the outset of this book is David Wiley, the chief academic officer of Lumen Learning, the education fellow at Creative Commons, and an adjunct faculty member at Brigham Young University, where he leads the Open Education Group. Wiley, who first coined the term "open content" in 1998, also authored *The Open Education Reader*, a collection of readings on open education with commentary. He has written and lectured extensively about open education technology and how the open education approach can help increase student success, improve teaching quality, and provide more equitable access to high-quality curricular materials. Wiley was an early adopter of key characteristics that are essential to Open Way Learning, such as establishing relationships of trust with students.

He allowed students the freedom to revise and remix the instructional OER to teach their peers through tutorials they created, provided frequent constructive feedback to students so they could iterate on their work, and created avenues for making the student work public. Such an approach sounds simple on its face, but, as Wiley has found, allowing students the autonomy to leverage the free reuse, revision, remixing, and redistribution of OER results in what he calls "insanely awesome student work."

The above examples illustrate the power of the Open Way movement in education. They provide the backstory for our approach. They also allude to something we found as we did the research for this book: the penetration of Open Way Learning approaches is still relatively small in the PK–12 space, at least relative to higher education. We believe this must change and have spent our collective careers developing a design to make that change happen in more schools and in more classrooms. The desire to share that model throughout the education ecosystem was the primary driver behind writing this book.

THE COMPONENTS OF OPEN WAY LEARNING

What should be obvious by now is that we firmly believe that the crowdsourced influence of the Open Way can catalyze pragmatic, intentional, local, and culturally responsive solutions that address our moral imperative for change. Both of our experiences and research have converged on the following insight: the path to sustainable success in any organization—education, industry, or otherwise—requires three seeds:

1. A culture of collaboration
2. Free exchange of knowledge
3. An innovation ethos

These three tenets rest on the foundation of shared vision and distributed leadership, as shown in figure 1.4.

This simple but powerful formula of essential characteristics, supported by practices and methods we will describe throughout the book, is what we call Open Way Learning (OWL). The remainder of the book will unpack this model and provide practical solutions and case studies to demonstrate its possibilities. It will also provide a clear vision of the Open Way Learning Academy, where all these components are being fully implemented.

What will compel educators to make such a fundamental change to be more collaborative, more open to sharing, and more inclined to innovate? The answer is having an open mind to the Open Way.

Just as software companies share their source code with competitors to elevate the entire industry, students and educators need to start sharing their ideas freely with each other. Keeping the best ideas in one classroom or in one student's head isolates those ideas from a community of innovators who could help optimize them. Like open-source coders, other teachers, students, administrators, and policy makers could modify the "source codes" of best practices for their own unique contexts and, in doing so, accelerate the pace of innovation to meet their own needs, for their own students and their own communities.

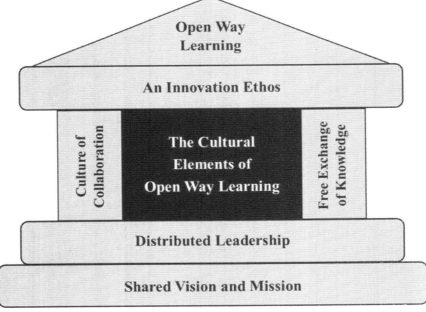

Figure 1.4.   The tenets of Open Way Learning are illustrated using a building metaphor.

Let's be clear: This will not be a cakewalk, as we learned when we interviewed and received feedback from hundreds of educators across the United States and elsewhere. While many were already using aspects of peer collaboration, free exchange of knowledge, and innovative practices to do amazing things with their students and in their schools, this tended to be scattered in pockets and not part of the mainstream. When pressed, many of these educators admitted either inconsistent or short-lived adoption of such practices. Many of those surveyed expressed frustration with a lack of genuine support (or even awareness) from their colleagues, administrators, and the bureaucratic systems in which they worked for why quality collaboration and trustful sharing of ideas and tools is necessary.

One former teacher of the year from Texas, who asked to remain anonymous, said her superintendent told her point blank: "We do not have enough time to do any of this [a proposal for more in-classroom peer collaboration] and also prepare our students for the state tests." This. Must. Change. In ecological systems and in business, stasis leads to extinction. One must constantly innovate to stay relevant to the needs of one's community or customers. The same is true in education.

We found evidence that elements of a movement exist to bring Open Way ideals to education. We also found relatively few people on the front lines of education who have a clear understanding of the array of open-source resources available to them. There are even fewer who understand how the open-source mindset can transform the fundamental power structure of the education ecosystem—from the individual classroom level to national policy.

With the specters of climate change, refugee crises, nuclear war, globalization, and automation looming over students' futures, they must be able to quickly adapt to changing circumstances by collaborating, freely exchanging knowledge, and then creatively innovating on other's ideas to devise novel solutions. This is a daunting challenge, and many would argue that we simply are not up to it. We respectfully disagree. Open Way Learning is an ideal way to help future generations practice essential skills that will make them potent changemakers in their fields of choice.

Questioning, challenging, and revamping the traditions and practices of the past to create the conditions for enough people to change their behavior, synthesize their work, and cross the tipping point for significant reform is possible, especially at the local level. The disruptive conditions of hyper-connectivity, free and open exchange of knowledge, and crowdsourced, technology-driven change have sparked massive improvements in essentially every aspect of our society—the time is ripe for these conditions to do the same in education.

OPEN EDUCATION RESOURCES (OER)

Many educators will already recognize the enormous value of bringing passion and engagement into the classroom to help students increase their depth of knowledge and take more responsibility for their own learning. Great principals are already working with their communities of learners to establish a respectful, trusting environment that leads to meritocracy-based decision-making and is consistent with the "code talks" mind-set. School board members may recognize the importance of strategies that enhance a participatory culture among a school's stakeholders: students, teachers, parents, and communities. Local businesses know the inherent economic value of having strong schools that are working in partnership with community leaders. We intend to show numerous examples from practitioners in the field who have benefited from the application of the core elements of the Open Way. In so doing, we will provide any education stakeholder a set of tools they can use to transform their own school through Open Way Learning.

The most obvious area to begin is within open education resources (OER). A large majority of the educators we interviewed expressed familiarity and experience with OER, even if they knew little else about the Open Way movement. Unsurprisingly, given its origins, there are several definitions of open education resources, but they all relate to educational materials that reside in the public domain or have been released under an open license that allows free access, reuse, revision, remixing, redistribution, and repurposing by others, with no restrictions or only limited restrictions (note that appendix 1 provides a historical summary of the OER movement).

The beauty of these resources is that they address the equity gap between well-funded schools and chronically underfunded schools. They also restore freedom of choice to the individual teacher or school so that they have free access to high-quality educational materials for students. The adoption of OER as an alternative to the traditional "pay to play" resources has even made its way into the policy arena, making it easier for districts to take advantage of the growing number of OER available each year.[9]

The growth of OER has been so prolific that it can be intimidating, especially for educators who have spent their careers relying on district-approved curricular materials or textbooks. Charlie Reisinger, open-sources advocate and school IT director for Penn Manor School District, has written a wonderful book called *The Open Schoolhouse* to address this issue. The easy-to-read guide uses his district as a case study in how anyone can optimize open technology. It provides step-by-step examples of how to make better use of open-source software, design an effective one-to-one technology policy, and, most impressively, form highly effective student help desk and student technology apprentice programs.

As we spoke to Charlie about *The Open Schoolhouse*, it became clear that he is both deeply knowledgeable and also passionate about helping any teacher, administrator, or technology director make significant improvements in their school or district's technology resources, all by taking advantage of more affordable open technologies and approaches that run counter to the typical stifling and controlling technology policies. We strongly encourage anyone serious about increasing the scope and scale of open-source resources to watch Charlie's video describing the amazing work he has led in his district.[10]

While *The Open Schoolhouse* focuses primarily on technology, other books have discussed the broader implications of the open revolution on teaching and learning. One example is David Price's *Open: How We'll Work, Live and Learn in the Future*. Price, whom we interviewed, is a leading education writer, speaker, and trainer and was awarded the Officer of the Order of the British Empire in 2009.

In *Open*, Price explains how the information age and social media have created not only an unprecedented level of open communication between people, but also an expectation of openness that challenges many traditional power structures. Using numerous case studies from within education, business, and government, he provides one of the clearest arguments for using open communication—especially in the form of social media platforms such as Twitter—to assert more authority over systems that have historically held the keys to change. With case studies from the School of Communication Arts 2.0 in London, England; the Sydney Centre for Innovation in Learning in Sydney, Australia; and High Tech High in San Diego, California, he also shows how teachers can enhance the teaching and learning environments for their students and both improve networking with peers and reshape the narrative in our often-maligned profession.

According to Brett Baker, account executive at Twitter.com, every day there are 4.2 million tweets related to education.[11] This means that for many teachers, the authors of this book included, Twitter offers a daily dose of inspiration and professional learning from peers connected to a worldwide virtual professional network. As Price puts it, these educator-driven virtual professional networks are "the biggest disruptive innovation to hit workplace learning in 50 years," and the implications are profound. Organizations are either learning how to embrace this new culture of connectedness or they are continuing to bury their heads in the sand, assuming it's a passing fad.

Being aware of technology and dabbling along the periphery is one thing. Being a connected educator means much more than having a professional social media presence or using the newest EdTech tools—open or otherwise—to make marginal improvements in what you were doing before. Without leveraging this wave of new technology to transform the teaching and learning systems in our schools, we acquiesce to passivity when what is needed is so much more. To put it bluntly, if the technology we are using in our schools is not fundamentally improving each student's chances in the global innovation economy, then we are not really changing the system.

Barnett Berry, the CEO of the Center for Teaching Quality, emphasized this point in his interview for this book: "[The Gates Foundation] estimates that a full one-third of all teachers are involved in some type of external network. This is the most groundswelling thing to happen to educational collaboration ever! The problem is that it's too episodic at this point. These are teachers who may be inclined to want to collaborate and share, but apart from a patchwork of success stories, we have not tapped into this vast network of educators as a virtual community of practice that is willing to reject the outdated practices of the past and embrace at scale what we know works for students."

INTENDED AUDIENCE, AIMS, AND APPROACH

One of the goals of this book is to provide anyone with a stake in education—from parents to educators to policy makers—with a clear picture of the open-source landscape and how it is positively disrupting closed systems and power structures worldwide. More importantly, however, the book aims to give the reader tangible entry points to be part of a movement. Without resorting to a paint-by-numbers approach, we describe clear, pragmatic actions anyone can employ using Open Way Learning methods to fundamentally change what they do and how they do it so that it better positions our schools to be incubators of unquestioned success.

At the same time, we are not naive enough to believe that this body of work will be a silver bullet to completely change the face of education in this country or any other. How we educate our children is simply too complex to be "reformed" by a single book or approach. Our primary focus is on education stakeholders who want an introduction to a new way of thinking and are willing to take concrete actions in their own classrooms, schools, districts, networks, and communities to see that change becomes a reality. We hope that includes you!

We took two primary approaches when writing this book: one was conducting a quasi meta-analysis and the other was gathering anecdotes from educators. This first approach was to cast a wide net into the body of research and literature both within education and elsewhere to identify the applicable tools, ideas, examples, and best practices that already resonate with the Open Way. Rather than rehashing already existing ideas for improving education, leadership, and organizational effectiveness, we have strategically analyzed, compiled, and synthesized these ideas and methods with an Open Way lens. At the same time, our examples are primarily focused on school governance, teacher leadership, and constructivist pedagogy—not all of which are explicit priorities for the current Open Way Learning movement.

Our second approach was to conduct interviews and gather input from practitioners—primarily educators—who could provide firsthand examples of how the key characteristics of an Open Way approach can be applied in schools. Our intent is not only to provide the reader with a holistic view through an Open Way lens of what has been proven to work (and not work) within and outside of education, but also to give practical advice anyone can adapt.

The book will take readers on a journey to implement some of these approaches by discussing how to instill an OWL culture and how to roll out the main components of collaboration, free knowledge, and innovation. It ends with a vision for an OWL academy based on our work in schools that shows how the elements of the OWL model work together. Stories of real teachers and thought leaders are woven throughout the book to highlight the work already underway to bring a more open approach to teaching children.

WHY THIS MATTERS NOW

Historically, information was available only for the privileged few. Books were exceedingly expensive, and education was reserved for the elite—mostly rich white males. Today, anyone with Internet access has an onramp to an endlessly updated tome of human knowledge that can help them accomplish almost any feat imaginable. They could learn harpsichord in the morning on YouTube, video conference with a programmer in Israel over lunch, then read peer-reviewed articles on medieval weaponry during the afternoon, only to watch a documentary on chocolate's social justice implications after dinner. It is mind-boggling how much knowledge is freely available to students in the digital age.

The didactic methods of the old school may have made sense in a historical context, although there is little evidence to justify their use.[12] In the past, teachers were truly the experts in the room and held precious knowledge that they generously imparted on their pupils, most often through lecture. They had access to realms of understanding strictly unavailable to their students, so it naturally follows that they would view students as receptacles to fill with their wisdom.

As the XQ Institute and the recent film *Most Likely to Succeed* both articulate, our schools are largely stuck in an antiquated, "prefactory" model, content to train students for a different place and a different time. In this traditional system, the best we can expect is that several well-supported students who have figured out how to play the game will be "successful" according to the narrowly defined measures of high test scores, graduating with a high school diploma, or getting into a good college. On the other end of the spectrum, however, too many of our students fall through the cracks. Any educator worth her or his salt knows that we can do better. So why don't we?

Given that Sir Ken Robinson's 2006 TED Talk, which asked, "Do Schools Kill Creativity?" is still the most viewed talk in the organization's history, one might then believe the societal will exists to do things differently.[13] But we still face an innate conservatism of public opinion that resists true education reform. We have seen this play out time and again at our school, where our innovative methods face consistent pushback because of the discomfort community members feel about our unorthodox approach. Rather than making the fundamental improvements needed to spawn a shift toward innovation over compliance and discovery over conformity, recent education reforms have directly or indirectly put standardized testing at the center of every teacher's universe.

Just as the old assembly line model for U.S. auto manufacturing became less efficient and reliance on it led to complacency that almost drove the Big Three U.S. automakers out of business, the public school model has also become complacent and comfortable and has long outgrown its usefulness. The result? A system that in many ways looks like it did a century ago. A system that needs an influx of new ideas and collective action to make them happen at scale.

We believe that education can only be improved for our students by rethinking what we have done in the past and embracing some relatively simple yet powerful and proven principles. Such a change, however, is not going to come from the outside. Investors, businesses, consultants, and philanthropists don't have the silver bullet or the moral authority to drive this change. Giving our students the education they deserve is going to come from within—from educators willing to trust that there is a better way. As society becomes less trustful of institutions, it becomes incumbent on those of us who are stewards of such institutions to adapt them to better fit the needs of our stakeholders.

INDUSTRY 3.0 AND BEYOND

Jeremy Rifkin, the American economic and social theorist, suggests in his 2011 book, *The Third Industrial Revolution*, that the very nature of the technological and information explosion that has driven this revolution is also leading to a fundamental transfer from hierarchical power to lateral power. This paradigm shift means the beneficiaries of the third industrial revolution are not necessarily large, multinational corporations, but entrepreneurs who can take advantage of the wealth of information at their fingertips and use it to create niche products and services they can sell directly to consumers via the online marketplace.[14]

As this third revolution evolves into what many are even calling a fourth industrial revolution made up of the Internet of Things, artificial intelligence, and cyberphysical systems, the ramifications on education are undeniable.[15] We can no longer equip our students with a minimum level of mathematical, scientific, language, and historical knowledge and then expect them to be successful.

The game has changed. A college degree—much less a high school diploma—no longer guarantees a job in the current global innovation economy. Instead of relying on credentials, anyone can take an idea to an online community, share and refine it, and then find collaborators to take it to the marketplace. One doesn't even have to rely on venture capitalists for funding ideas. As Peter Norvig, director of research at Google, points out, "One of the best programmers I ever hired had only a high school degree; he's produced a lot of great software, has his own news group, and made enough in stock options to buy his own nightclub." Moreover, with crowdfunding sites such as Kickstarter, GoFundMe, RocketHub, and Indiegogo, any savvy entrepreneur can find the financial backing needed to get a start-up idea off the ground.

Heather McGowan, cofounder of Work to Learn, succinctly describes why this matters now: "In the future, those who continuously learn will continue to lead." She then reinforces that point by saying that in the future education will shift from "a content transfer to learning as a continuous process where the focused outcome is the ability to learn and adapt with agency as opposed to the transactional action of acquiring a set skill."[16]

Society is evolving to a point at which every job that hasn't been automated will require constantly growing technical skills in a fundamentally different way than was required in the past. That new reality means that schools must make creative and complex critical thinking a daily reality if they are truly preparing students for a world that thrives on and rewards innovation. That paradigm shift cannot wait. It must begin now.

Meanwhile, young people are increasingly anxious about their future prospects. The GenForward Survey, run out of the University of Chicago, is a nationally representative survey of over 1,750 young adults between the ages of eighteen and thirty-four and is conducted bimonthly.[17] It found that a relatively high number of millennials across racial and ethnic groups believe that advances in technology will decrease the number of available jobs, with higher levels of concern in Asian American (51 percent), African American

(48 percent), and Latino (46 percent) respondents, as compared to White respondents (35 percent).

This points to a level of discomfort and uncertainty—perhaps stemming from inadequate preparation—even among our young people who should feel most confident about their future. Where does the responsibility for preparation lie? To a large extent, it rests in the K–12 education system. Educators must prioritize giving our young people the skills to enter this uncertain world with confidence, thus taking advantage of, instead of ignoring, this third revolution. Isolating oneself in one's classroom and assuming it will somehow all work out is not the answer.

We must demand that the spoon-fed, didactic, content-focused model be flipped on its head. That students, as well as teachers and administrators, constantly tackle the many ill-defined problems where there is no proverbial correct answer in the back of the book. That students not only master curricular content, but do so by developing practical skills such as entrepreneurship, global awareness, critical thinking, and communication. That we restructure schools by eliminating the calcified hierarchical structure in favor of one that is flatter, more inclusive, and better networked.

We also must extend the classroom beyond the school walls by expanding learning into the local and global community, where students see direct purpose and passion in learning by doing. When we take a different path through these and other efforts, we once and for all take seriously the goal of making every student a lifelong learner for a world that demands it.

Open Way tools and mindsets have been proven to work, both inside and outside of education contexts. They challenge the assumptions of the past and help us to better deliver nimble, high-quality, just-in-time instruction customized to the individual growth of each student. By using this approach, we can finally say with confidence that we are achieving the lofty and unique goals set forth in the original mission of our public education system. If that's your goal as an education stakeholder, then we welcome you to the critical mass that will create the cultural tipping point we desperately need. Roll up your sleeves and read on.

2

Planting Open Way Learning Seeds

It's the essence of our humanity—to create, to invent, to make our world better.—Ted Dintersmith, author of *What School Could Be: Insights and Inspiration from Teachers across America*

Before Open Way Learning can take root in any organization, three fundamental cultural principles must be in place: collaboration, free knowledge, and an innovation mindset. These principles cannot be established until the hoarding and isolation of knowledge are understood and remediated. Only then will openness become the default culture. Why might educators gravitate to a closed-minded mentality, and how can a member of this disempowering ecosystem shift toward a more productive path of openness and trust?

Interestingly, when an environment becomes competitive and dangerous in the natural world, similar strategies emerge. Tropical ecosystems are known for intense biological competition. When faced with this competition, some species begin to hide, become nocturnal or highly specialized, develop poisons, or hoard their food resources and anxiously defend them. More behaviorally flexible and intelligent species establish alliances with one another and learn to cooperate in mutualistic ways.

Some squirrels, for example, practice larder hoarding, where they stash all their food for winter in one big pile. They spend the rest of their time fiercely defending their mound of pinecones by raising the alarm at anything that comes in sight. This can be a successful strategy, but it certainly keeps them vulnerable to thieves and constantly afraid—surviving, but not thriving.

In contrast, the mongooses and the hornbills in the Taru Desert of Kenya have developed an unlikely alliance. The hornbills actually wake the mongooses each morning so they can begin foraging in the tall grasses surrounding their burrows. As the furry foragers race through the grass looking for breakfast, they stir up insects for their winged partners in crime to eat. Meanwhile, the hornbills use their high-angle vantage points to act as sentinels for the mongooses, sounding an alarm anytime they see potential predators. Thanks to the nuanced interspecies communication patterns they've developed, the mongooses understand which predator is approaching and take the appropriate escape route!

Education in the twenty-first century is analogous to a tropical ecosystem. The extreme competition between classrooms, schools, districts, states, and nations is enough to make any educator want to retreat into relative safety behind the locked classroom door. Indeed, many educators "squirrel" away their best resources to maintain a competitive edge against colleagues. There, they can avoid being "devoured" by a dissatisfied parent, policy maker, administrator, or student. Students are also increasingly aware of the amplified competition for placement in today's colleges and workplaces.

In the documentary *2 Million Minutes*, filmmakers contrast how students in the United States, India, and China spend their high school years. It vividly displays how competition between students affects the chances they have to be accepted at their schools of choice. Such ubiquitous, competition-induced fear can quickly infect schools by creating seemingly intractable systems where no one wants to risk failure.

It is becoming obvious that some of our so-called reform efforts that directly or indirectly encourage competition are not in the best interests of students or educators. Jeffrey Mirel and Simona Goldin cite an example in their 2012 article for the *Atlantic*: "If teachers are competing with one another for merit pay, why should they collaborate with one another? They might as well go back behind their closed doors."[1]

The methodology of Open Way Learning runs directly counter to this unhealthy emphasis on competition and emerges from a culture of openness embedded in the fabric of the organization. This is nonnegotiable. Without a deep level of organizational trust and mutual respect between members of the learning community, it's not really Open Way Learning. Moreover, creating the right environment for Open Way Learning to occur must be a community effort emerging from a truly shared vision.

To steer the ocean liner that is public education in the right direction, educators need to start thinking like hornbills and mongooses. Without collaboration, the free sharing of knowledge, and an innovative mindset, all based on a shared vision and leadership, true Open Way Learning will not exist. This chapter describes what is needed for these essential elements of OWL—the cultural seeds—to take root and thrive.

SEED 1: COLLABORATION

Imagine for a moment that you are interviewing for a new teaching position at two different schools, School A and School B. Your research into both schools suggests that they each have solid community and parental support, state-of-the-art facilities, and above-average test scores.

Upon visiting each school for the on-site interview, however, you find that they are significantly different. School A has a very controlling environment and a rigid, hierarchical organization. Teachers keep their doors closed and locked, rules are posted throughout the building, and students walk quietly through the halls, avoiding eye contact and always being accompanied by teachers to keep them in line. The classrooms are all very neat and relatively calm, with students busily working independently or listening to instructions from their teachers.

You meet the principal, and, although she is very busy, she takes a few minutes to ask you detailed questions about your classroom management style, your subject matter expertise, and what you can do to help her improve the school's test scores. She says in a very matter-of-fact manner that she will be in touch with you later in the week and asks her administrative assistant to escort you out the front door.

By contrast, you find a very open and warm atmosphere at School B. Everyone greets you with a welcoming smile, and the teachers all express how much they love working there because of the autonomy and voice they are given in meeting the school's shared mission and goals. You are interviewed by a team of teachers and students, and although you meet the principal while visiting one of the open classrooms, she has delegated complete trust and hiring authority to this team. Rather than rules, you see an abundance of student work and motivational statements posted throughout the building.

The team encourages you to step into as many classrooms as you wish, and you find each to be lively, with students engaged in a variety of collaborative activities, yet also eager to share with you what they are doing. Instead of questions about test scores, the interview team asks that you provide examples of how you encourage mindfulness, develop strong relationships with your students and peers, and use those efforts to promote a growth mindset. The team takes the time to answer each of your questions and promises to let you know something as soon as possible. Two students enthusiastically volunteer to help you find your way back to the front door and thank you for your visit.

Two days later you receive offers from both schools. Here's the catch: while both offers have generous pay and benefits, School A's has a significantly higher salary. What do you do? While your answer would obviously depend on your specific situation, there is a growing body of evidence that many candidates, especially today's millennials, would sacrifice higher pay to work in a collaborative environment where their voice matters.

Rob Asghar, in his 2014 article for *Forbes*, "What Millennials Want in the Workplace (And Why You Should Start Giving It to Them)," points to research done by Jamie Gutfreund, chief marketing officer for the award-winning global digital agency Deep Focus.[2] She says that millennials are "not looking to fill a slot in a faceless company. They're looking strategically at opportunities to invest in a place where they can make a difference, preferably a place that itself makes a difference." In other words, they want to collaborate, share ideas, and have their voices heard from day one.

> Take a room full of five-year-olds and you will see creativity in all its forms positively flowing around the room. A decade later you will see these same children passively sitting at their desks, half asleep or trying to decipher what will be on the next test.—Madeline Levine, author of *Teach Your Children Well*

So, what happens when schools across the nation refuse to acknowledge this trend by actively or indirectly discouraging collaboration? Teacher shortages. A recent report by the U.S. Department of Education's Teacher Shortage Areas indicates school districts across the United States are facing significant challenges attracting and retaining high-quality teachers.[3] While base teacher pay certainly contributes to this looming epidemic, working conditions are another significant factor.

Teachers entering today's workforce are less tolerant of a workplace where they are told what to do, where their voices are either unheard or underappreciated, where there are few opportunities for professional growth and collaboration with peers to solve problems. When compounded with low pay, inconsistent administrative support, excessive paperwork, the pressures of standardized testing, and metrics that may not accurately measure a teacher's true worth, is it any wonder schools have difficulty retaining high-quality teachers?

The good news is that we also know what works, and it looks a lot like our hypothetical School B! What educator would not want to work in such a school? In addition to creating a powerful environment for student learning, the Open Way ethos in School B will be attractive to anyone who expects to do her or his life's work in an atmosphere that values the free flow of ideas, seeks the chance for leadership development and growth, and expects open collaboration between peers. Given that teachers are generally undervalued and underpaid, the gap between the demand and supply of highly qualified teachers is expected to grow unless some of these structural changes are made and baseline pay is raised.[4] After all, great teachers are imperative for preparing our children for the future. Shouldn't that be valued appropriately?

> Working hard for something we don't care about is called stress; working hard for something we love is called passion.—Simon Sinek, author of *Start with Why*

Here's the bottom line: the traditional organizational model neither nurtures dynamic innovation nor responds quickly to the needs of its community. As a result, it is not attractive to the current and developing workforce. We can either accept this reality or continue to see the gap widen between the supply of teachers and the demand in our schools. By rethinking our educational models to encourage an open culture of collaboration, free sharing of knowledge and ideas, and frequent opportunities for professional growth, we can make our schools attractive to the next generation of great teachers who will prepare our students for the work valued in today's innovation economy. One of the best opportunities for change is within a powerful professional learning community where OWL can flourish.

High Stakes, Low Collaboration

Federal policies such as No Child Left Behind and Race to the Top (RTTT), while well intended, have not incentivized teacher-led collaboration. These initiatives certainly resulted in some positive outcomes—turning around low-performing schools, furthering the adoption of standards and assessments that better prepare students to succeed in college and career, and generally improving teacher and principal effectiveness—but other improvements are less clear.[5]

Many teachers would also suggest that regulatory initiatives such as RTTT have only exacerbated the problem of teacher isolation. In many cases, they have led to more distrust, as evidenced by Elaine Weiss in a 2013 report she did for the Economic Policy Institute.[6] In it, Weiss explains, "The heavy focus on evaluation and punishment over improvement has made teachers, principals, and superintendents suspicious and has reduced support for RTTT."

Case in point: teacher evaluations, if done well, can be a way to significantly improve teaching effectiveness and quality at a school. Unfortunately, evaluations quickly done by overwhelmed administrators to satisfy a bureaucratic check box are inadequate. Incomplete or inaccurate feedback not only undermines trust between the teacher and administrators but can lead to greater teacher isolation, unhealthy competition between teachers, and fear of arbitrary retribution.

High-stakes testing has added another obstacle to openness in schools. A teacher working in a large school with multiple versions of the same class may feel threatened by other teachers of their subject. A logical reaction to this threat would be to hoard their best methods and resources to maintain a competitive edge over their peers—just like the squirrel defending their larder. They may also develop the unproductive habit of teaching to the test. Administrators and policy makers compelled by the OWL methodology would do well to deemphasize testing as the predominant indicator of teaching quality, especially if they want their students to remain globally competitive. In fact, the OWL framework focuses primarily on the development of skills and processes that students will use for the rest of their lives as opposed to simply helping them pass a test to measure content knowledge.

Let's be clear. There is value in having transparent and accurate systems for accountability in our schools, to measure both teacher performance and student mastery of essential content. Six Sigma methodology, for example, emphasizes that organizations should "measure what drives the right behavior."[7] Accountability systems, however, can be misused and drive unintended outcomes such as less collaboration, more unhealthy competition, and an unhealthy focus on test preparation over true learning.[8]

We also know that, paradoxically, students tend to develop and retain more content knowledge when they are truly engaged in activities that connect curricular topics to things they care about.[9] A more balanced approach, one that can thrive in an OWL framework, is for administrators to frequently remind teachers that solid exam scores are but one of many instructional goals and that employment decisions are based on a wide range of criteria as opposed to a single test score. Doing this will help remedy a toxic dynamic that leads to closed doors and closed minds.

Counterproductive Competition

In Alfie Kohn's famous and controversial book *No Contest*, he evaluates hundreds of examples to make the point that "healthy competition" is not only a contradiction in terms but is doing more harm than good in education. This body of work suggests that rather than motivating us to excel, competition undermines relationships, productivity, and self-esteem. Kohn cites a review of 122 studies on the question of competition. Of these, "65 studies found that cooperation promotes higher achievement than competition, eight found the reverse, and 36 found no statistically significant difference." So while it would be naive to suggest that the deep-rooted culture of competition in our schools can be eliminated or even reduced, we must reject its damaging influence on professional, peer-to-peer collaboration.

Unfortunately, many of the teacher evaluation systems currently being used encourage competition and undermine teacher collaboration. Teachers should be fairly evaluated and held accountable to high expectations, but the current system does not take advantage of one of the most significant indicators of student success: collaboration.[10] Moreover, a recent article in the *Guardian* indicates that in the UK there has been a growing realization on both ends of the political spectrum that the emphasis on hyperfocused competition is misguided.[11]

Interschool rivalries can be as damaging as misapplied systems for evaluation and testing. Though some "good old-fashioned hate" can be useful on the football field, it has no place in our classrooms. Some will argue that healthy competition can motivate students and teachers, but when that competition diminishes collaboration and fails to benefit students, it has crossed a line. Perhaps it goes against everything you believe in, but there is a good chance that you have something to learn from any teacher you interact with, especially when you put aside the differences you established or you let society establish for you. What does that mean? Public schools learning from charters, private school teachers learning from public school teachers, and policy makers learning from teachers.

Instead of allowing misguided rivalry and competition to undermine the open sharing of ideas, solutions, and success stories, we should be attending to the broader mission of all schools to prepare students to thrive in the twenty-first century. As cliché as it sounds, all educators are in this together and should be striving to enable every student to maximize his or her potential to meet the needs of society and to become a lifelong learner in an ever-changing world. Competition inside the school or between schools should never distract from this overarching educational aim.

A Bedrock of Trust

Is it any wonder, given the stark realities described above, that Open Way Learning seeds fall on infertile ground? Why would anyone in such an environment want to step out of the comfort zone of what has been traditionally accepted as "good teaching," especially when they have little to no exposure to innovative teaching practices that may be happening in the room next door? It's hard for even the most passionate OWL educator to make headway in a system that demands compliance over trust. He or she is often left to retreat to safe, status quo teaching methods.

If you have been in education long enough, you know that the popular answer to the question "Why did you become a teacher?" is "To make a difference." Yet making a difference requires a big dose of different! Teachers taking chances must start with a bedrock of trust, where an emphasis on collaboration is at the core. If educators and their students do not sense that deep commitment to trust and view collaboration as paramount, then they will never feel safe to try something as innovative as it is effective.

LESSONS FROM MANUFACTURING

Perhaps education could learn from the history of manufacturing. In the twentieth century, the U.S. manufacturing sector was undergoing major changes due to an emerging global marketplace. Companies were weighing the benefits and drawbacks of globalization, outsourcing, free trade, and automation. Ben was witness to this as an engineer for a multinational chemical company, responsible for finding ways to increase production, reliability, and quality, all while adhering to strict safety and environmental requirements. Through this process, he learned organizations could only remain viable and relevant in a competitive industry if they moved away from a traditional (and expensive) hierarchical model to one that was lean, nimble, and based on mission-driven distributed leadership.

In this model, rather than having to wait for bureaucratic management to tell every employee what was needed for every situation, everyone in the organization was expected to bring their ideas to the table and actively solve problems. They arrived at solutions by bringing their unique skills and perspectives to bear on each problem that would arise, and they were then empowered to make just-in-time decisions that drove continuous improvement.

This self-directed workforce meant that every member of the organization was an equal, respected stakeholder constantly collaborating with his or her peers to make decisions that helped meet mission-critical needs. Were mistakes made? Yes. Yet mistakes were understood. Ignoring a problem or refusing to seek input from peers to help solve that problem was grounds for demotion or dismissal. To this day, many of the companies who weathered this transition still provide meaningful work and economic benefits for the communities where they thrive.

The education space can be significantly different than the context of other professions, and just because something works in the private sector does not always mean that it will translate into improving outcomes for children. Students are not widgets, and every educator is likely able to point to examples of corporations that take advantage of taxpayer dollars intended to help students and schools. Nevertheless, one of the pillars of any open and collaborative organizational structure is that it must trust and empower every member of that organization to be a decision maker. Regardless of whether the organization is in the private sector or within education, unless the leadership is willing to forgo the controlling, top-down structure to embrace mission-driven collective autonomy, that organization's days are numbered.

Enough Already!

Admittedly, most of what has been mentioned up to now in this chapter paints a rather bleak picture of our educational systems. This does not mean all hope is lost! High-quality collaboration between educators does exist, if only in scattered pockets that have yet to coalesce into a critical mass where Open Way Learning can thrive.

Without a not-so-gentle nudge, the institutionalized inertia of our massive education system is quite content to perpetuate the status quo. The good news is that there are ways you can—individually or with a team—begin to build the case for why that nudge needs to occur now. Moreover, you can help your local school and the larger educational system reach the tipping point to better collaboration and OWL excellence.

Many schools have the building blocks of what can, with a lot of work and nurturing, evolve into collaborative professional learning communities that provide the framework for routine, open sharing of ideas. Examples of such highly effective teacher collaboration models include Critical Friends Groups that lead to trust-based feedback and support focused on improving instruction and student learning;[12] Lesson Study, where teachers follow a methodical approach developed by Japanese teachers to examine and improve each other's teaching practices;[13] and "bottom-up" decision-making models such as the Teacher-Powered School model described in the 2016 book by Evers and Kneyber titled *Flip the System: Changing Education from the Ground Up.* These are but a sampling of powerful models that rely on collaboration, openness, trust, and a growth mindset. And while their success depends on several factors, each assumes that every member of a school's organization is valued and respected as they individually and collectively strive to live up to their own shared vision of excellence.

Imagine being part of School B's learning community for a moment. Or, better yet, imagine being part of an entire district or region made up of such schools. Schools where a culture of mutual respect and trust pervades every decision and drives individual and collective growth for all stakeholders. Schools that enable collaborative networks to thrive and make quick and nimble decisions based on the facts at hand so that short-term and long-term goals are attained at an optimum pace. Schools where improvements in student equity are achieved through personalized engagement and where redefined leadership roles and the use of appropriate metrics lead to more flexible, adaptive solutions that drive improvements in student outcomes. Such schools embody the essence of Open Way Learning.

How do you create such a school, where collaboration is its lifeblood? This book provides plenty of ideas, especially in chapter 3, where we take a deep dive into how to implement and scale recognized collaborative best practices that have been proven to work. Before that, let's return to our second seed, the free sharing of knowledge.

SEED 2: FREE KNOWLEDGE

The OWL framework is predicated on openly sharing knowledge. Freeing knowledge can occur on multiple levels, but it starts in the classroom. Teachers must acknowledge their role as curators and interpreters of infinitely accessible knowledge and reject the idea of being the sole proprietor of knowledge in the room. Moreover, connected teachers benefit from the significant network effects of sharing their own information and accessing other colleagues' resources from around the world. In short, moving away from hoarding knowledge and toward open and free sharing is another nonnegotiable practice to fully embody the Open Way Learning philosophy.

Here is another example outside of education that illustrates the power behind the free exchange of knowledge. While it may seem counterintuitive, Japanese automaker Toyota shares its philosophies and practices with other companies, including their own competitors. In fact, they entered a joint venture with General Motors in the early 1980s at the New United Motor Manufacturing facility in Fremont, California.

Why would they do that? As Jeffrey Liker states in his 2004 book, *The Toyota Way: 14 Management Principles from the World's Greatest Manufacturer*, one consideration was the belief that by helping the world's largest car maker—General Motors—which at the time was struggling to remain competitive, they were helping society and the community at large. If publicly traded companies such as Toyota can collaborate and share ideas within their market to raise the standard of manufacturing excellence, shouldn't educators be able to more freely share ideas, resources, and best practices within education? This is, after all, an entire profession focused on teaching and growing the next generation so its members can thrive as productive citizens in the future!

To further highlight the value of the free exchange of knowledge, consider the medical profession, where freely exchanging knowledge and resources is expected. Imagine you're in your doctor's office and hear him say that he has no value for the articles published in the *New England Journal of Medicine* or the *Journal of the American Medical Association*. He knows everything he needs to know based on the twenty-five years he's been in the medical profession and has no time to go to professional conferences or to chat with his peers about what's new on the horizon. You would probably be seeking a new doctor that same day!

SURPRISED BY SHARING

Ben often shares a story from early in his teaching career. He was at a large education convention in Washington, D.C., where he had the opportunity to meet teachers from across the country and to work on a task with them. Ben was just embarking on using project-based learning in his math class and offered these new teacher friends his flash drive so that they could have access to all his projects and supporting resources. Each of these teachers gladly accepted the drive and eagerly made copies for themselves, but they all acted somewhere between surprised and appalled that Ben would so willingly share what had obviously taken him months of hard work to develop. One person even admitted that he would never do this type of sharing in his own department because it could lead him to be ranked below one of his peers. He said that he always kept his hard-earned resources to himself in order to have a competitive advantage over his colleagues.

Fortunately, the scenario at the doctor's office would almost certainly never occur. Unfortunately, you may very likely find at least one teacher who takes this shortsighted view in a school in your own community. We'll call him Mr. Changeless. The administration may even rate Mr. Changeless as a "distinguished teacher" based on the methods he employs to consistently get high test scores from his students. In fact, why should Mr. Changeless change, given that under the current narrow definitions of student success, he is achieving satisfactory results?

Teachers Helping Teachers

Mr. Changeless developed his resource materials ten years ago and keeps them locked in a filing cabinet until he teaches the relevant unit. He hasn't even updated them because that would be too laborious and his students perform well enough on the state-mandated final exams. In fact, his state hasn't updated the standards for the last decade either! "If it ain't broke, don't fix it," basically sums up his teaching philosophy. Meanwhile, Ms. Freemarket has been posting all of her best original resources online for purchase and earns a few hundred dollars a year from her sales. She feels that teacher pay is way too low, so she needs to have a "side hustle." "Have my cake and eat it too" was her favorite phrase last year as she shared her entrepreneurial scheme with colleagues.

Finally, Mr. N. O. Vader frequently participates in Twitter chats, regularly uses resources from other teachers, and freely shares his practices on his website and various social media channels. He tends to be a vocal leader at teacher meetings and has been responsible for various outside-the-box teaching initiatives implemented by the school over the last few years. He has also been called an overachiever by some of his peers.

Administrators eager to cultivate the OWL mindset at their school need to ensure that practices like Mr. Vader's become the model for the teachers at the school. While Ms. Freemarket's strategy should be encouraged to a degree, it creates a barrier through its price tag. Teachers in many areas certainly need higher compensation, and the profession suffers from a lack of respect by some policy makers and members of society at large. That, however, is a topic for another book. The reality is that with the explosion of open education resources and with the growing number of Mr. Vaders out there who are eager to freely share anything they have developed as long as it helps other teachers improve, Ms. Freemarket's approach becomes less relevant.

Mr. Vader's free knowledge orientation has made him a better teacher and has helped other teachers in his network build stronger and more engaging learning opportunities for their students. Rather than keeping his best resources locked away or selling them, he announces to any and all that they may take what he has done and improve it. As you recall from chapter 1, this ethos has not only fueled Silicon Valley as an economic and innovative dynamo but is at the heart of the Open Way. His generosity also creates a karmic reciprocity where others are more likely to share with him. Ultimately, this strategy improves the entire educational ecosystem and has the transforming potential to improve the perception of public schools over time, because it advertises innovative teaching methods that are laser-focused on student success.

Consequently, teacher respect and pay could increase, as is the case in Finland.[14] Moreover, career prospects for teachers like Mr. Vader increase because his organization recognizes his leadership without his needing to leave the classroom. Moreover, his sense of purpose in his profession, both locally and beyond, is reinforced through the open sharing of ideas that he helps enable. In essence, he's playing the long game because he has a passion for excellence.

Planting the seeds for OWL means identifying these teachers and other forward-thinking leaders in your or your community's school or district and amplifying their free-sharing influence by applauding their efforts and celebrating their methods. By highlighting, synthesizing, and leveraging the behind-the-scenes leadership these people have over the free exchange of ideas and resources, you make your learning community more open, transparent, and effective. This may be difficult if you are fighting an entrenched culture where such sharing is considered to be unnecessary "rocking the boat." Each educator will need to reconsider his or her fundamental roles in the free knowledge landscape to truly open up such teaching and nontraditional leadership practices. In short, if you are not enabling this kind of free sharing in your own local context, it's time to rock the boat.

Jason Sickle, a science teacher at Mountain Vista High School in Highlands Ranch, Colorado, describes how he and his fellow physics teachers collaborate at his school using Google Apps for Education (GAFE) in an open sharing framework:

> There are five of us teaching physics, and we all use a modeling approach with resources provided by Arizona State University. . . . All five of us organize and share these resources through a Google Drive and are continually updating, modifying, and tweaking what we use and how we use it. We are often in each other's classroom, either learning from each other or team teaching. We're also constantly updating and sharing our own respective class websites and have concentrated our resources and equipment into one area of the building to better facilitate easy sharing. At the end of the day, we all work hard to maintain a sharing culture simply because we know it helps make us all better teachers for our students.

Ernie Rambo, a veteran world geography, physical science, English, and history teacher in the Clark County School District in Las Vegas, Nevada, provides this anecdote about how she and her colleagues were able to grow collaborative, open sharing in their school:

> For three years, content area teachers had been collaborating on setting goals and discussing progress. When our faculty met for staff development, the content area teachers had common understandings that the electives and [physical education] did not share. We wanted to be part of the content teachers' efforts, and our principal showed that she understood that by working with the entire staff to develop ways for us all to collaborate and share ideas that were consistent with the common good of the entire school. . . . This example highlights how teachers' observations and willingness to do something about it set in motion a solution that worked.

In another example, a team of passionate educators scaled collaboration and free sharing across the school. Boston Day and Evening Academy in Boston, Massachusetts, does a project each year during Thanksgiving and winter break, during which teachers coteach one interdisciplinary class for a group of self-selected students every day, all day for the six weeks. It is a deep dive

A CHALLENGE

Put the book down for a moment and grab a pencil and piece of paper. Write down as many examples as you can from your professional career where a lack of clear communication and open exchange of knowledge led to more work on your part, a misunderstanding that affected your morale or that of your team, or a crisis—real or perceived—that could have otherwise been avoided. Now list some simple ways your organization or the people in your sphere of influence could shift focus toward sharing and transparency to avoid such issues. It's likely that several of the situations you wrote down affected students' lives, and time and energy were spent repairing the damage rather than changing the opportunity trajectory for these children. How will you respond to this challenge?

into the subjects, where the whole process is about collaboration and open sharing between teachers and students.

Great educators know that to be part of a great school, they must have a tenacious focus on excellence by working every day with their peers to create and nurture a culture of open, transparent sharing of ideas and resources that helps everyone in the learning community improve their performance. It means finding ways to share the things you see and know to work with peers at the department, in your building, and across the district. It means challenging the assumptions behind the disempowering statement "we can't do that" by sharing solution-focused ideas within professional networks, both face-to-face and virtual. It also means strengthening the sharing environment by openly and freely showing how one uses what is learned to make classrooms better places for learning.

When built on a foundation of trusting collaboration, the free exchange of ideas will make such organizations more effective. The biggest mistake you can make is to underestimate the power of a team of teaching and learning experts with the passion and capacity to remove the barriers to collaborative, free exchange of knowledge. That is the true power of open-source sharing, and it unleashes unprecedented innovation.

Chapter 4 further elaborates on the ideal uses of free knowledge for the benefit of educators and students by delving into resources and techniques used by OWL practitioners. Both collaboration and free knowledge can push the needle toward a culture that embraces the Open Way, but this philosophy will never realize its full potential without an innovative mindset from all stakeholders in an organization.

SEED 3: INNOVATIVE MINDSETS

Innovation is part and parcel with going down blind alleys.—Jeff Bezos, CEO of Amazon

The last essential seed for any OWL network to take root is a culture of innovation, which must be a core value of every member in the organization. We are living through the sixth mass extinction event in our planet's history. Paleontologists and biologists widely agree that dramatic environmental changes underlie most of these events. Asteroids, ice ages, and climate change have all been culprits in the past, and it appears that one of those will be chiefly responsible for this one as well. However, not all species are affected in the same way. Those most capable of rapid adaptation tend to have the best prospects. Our friends the mongoose and hornbill exemplify the innovative behavioral adaptations that can arise for the more social and intelligent species. These are the types of adaptations that will ultimately give those species a fighting chance in this unpredictable era. If they're lucky and establish more unlikely alliances and take advantage of unusual opportunities, they may avoid extinction.

The global economic ecosystem is undergoing its own sea change; dramatic swings have led to countless bankruptcies and generations of perplexed workers who watched their jobs shipped offshore or automated. Meanwhile, numerous businesses are resisting change and falling prey to disruptors that invaded their niche and put them out of business. Think Uber, Airbnb, and Netflix, with their enormous effects on taxi drivers, hotels, and video stores—they're the invasive species of the economy.

It is time that schools embrace their own positive disruptors—that is, the fearless innovators—rather than sending them to the principal's office! Students graduating from schools across the globe are inheriting a world of uncertainty and constant change. Schools, unions, administrations, policy makers, and education departments who truly understand this believe what they are doing today is not good enough for tomorrow. Those who do not innovate, whether they realize it or not, are headed down the path of irrelevance. Organizations must prepare students to create their own alliances, exploit opportunities, and adapt to an ever-changing world. In other words, they must be ready to innovate early and often if they want to avoid extinction in the digital age.

Open = Innovation

The term "innovation" has become so overused in education that it has essentially lost its meaning. Don't think so? Google "innovative worksheet" and see the number of results. Go to any education conference and you are apt to see vendors lined up selling all kinds of "innovative" products and services to help students, teachers, and administrators improve how they do what they do. If you examine these "innovative" products and services closely, most are existing products repackaged with new bells and whistles and a shiny new veneer. This is especially true in the EdTech arena, where many products are specifically designed to fit within the deeply entrenched lexicon of "doing school" using the industrialized methods we've always used. Granted, there are some exceptions, but an unnamed contributor to this book who used to work for a large educational resource firm admitted that their offerings could not be too far from the prevailing teacher-centered model because the market for anything else is simply not large enough to support the required investment. It's a sad testament to the philosophy of knowing one's audience.

True innovation is not superficial. It comes from an intense cycle of collaborative iteration, where members of a team are constantly sharing new ideas and knowledge based on what has been done before so that they can do it better. Yet as important as collaboration and free sharing are to an Open Way Learning environment, by themselves they are not enough. There has to be a method to the madness! Without an intentional and methodical process, collaboration loses its potency and becomes glorified socialization, and sharing becomes haphazard.

Ted Fujimoto, a consultant who helped found New Tech and Big Picture Learning schools, mentioned his reticence about relying too heavily on teachers sharing best practices because all sharing isn't necessarily high quality. According to Fujimoto, the key is being methodical in the process of engineering a school model rather than "hacking" innovative school models. Basing school models on the raw materials mined from the collaborative, open sharing culture requires careful curation, then artful compilation and refinement of those raw materials before OWL will really thrive. Thus, school teams must think like innovative engineers to find successful practices for their students in their context.

As mentioned in chapter 1, the original open-source ideology was founded on the principle of innovation. Programmers would open up their work to the scrutiny of other coders who would build on that initial code. Educators hoping to embody this mindset will have to take cues from the coders' playbook. Like the computer programmers who originated the concept, educators will need to be aware of and informed about the work of other educators.

Instead of developing all their own original lesson plans while isolated in their classrooms, they will become experts in taking already created materials and retrofitting them for use in their own unique context. Like doctors, lawyers, engineers, and other professionals, educators will need to be well-versed on the latest developments applicable to their work. This includes best practices and research, as well as policy changes and local developments that impact their students. Just as in the case of the programmer who continues to develop and refine her coding expertise through collaborative debugging and rapid prototyping, this real-time professional development allows educators to become better contributors to the work of a school or group of schools. They will then make their work available for others to see and adapt as needed in new classrooms. This cycle repeats itself via the engineering design process and becomes a simple yet powerful formula at the core of a culture of innovation.

> People can have two different mindsets. . . . [T]hose with a "fixed mindset" believe that their talents and abilities are carved in stone. Those with a "growth mindset" believe that their talents and abilities can be developed. Fixed mindsets see every encounter as a test of their worthiness. Growth mindsets see the same encounters as opportunities to improve.—Carol Dweck, Lewis and Virginia Eaton Professor of Psychology at Stanford University

When applied in an Open Way Learning environment, teaching and learning practices such as mastery- or competency-based learning, problem- and project-based learning, place-based service learning, and the like become more potent because they are under the constant scrutiny of a collaborative team of passionate educators focused on deeper learning for everyone in their learning community. This community of educators is then willing to take an unflinching approach to developing, refining, and improving new innovations—whether developed in-house or elsewhere—and aligning them with a long-term goal of ensuring every student will graduate ready for success in college, careers, and life. Real success, not pretend success just because it's written on a largely ignored mission statement.

This innovation dynamic creates rippling network effects that ultimately lead to better resources, methods, and relationships for educators worldwide, which naturally cascades into improved student outcomes. It also streamlines many typical tasks of a teacher that can interrupt the ability to invest in student relationships and do creative thinking. To be fair, the constant demands of planning, grading, and extracurricular duties tax many educators and leave them so exhausted that imagining inventive new practices becomes unappealing.

Therefore, OWL educators are never ashamed to borrow strategies, methods, and resources from others instead of laboriously reinventing the wheel. Their work then becomes more efficient and effective. They become adept at navigating the virtual firehose of educational knowledge on the web, curating the best of the best to meet the specific needs of each of their students.

Their true originality comes from the unique combinations of resources they compile and the personal spin they put on them. For instance, one teacher's mundane worksheets can become a "scaffolding" choice for an OWL teacher's project-based learning unit, enabling students to build an adequate depth of knowledge as they work to complete a compelling final product.

Jason H. Parker, a youth job development manager and Startup Weekend global facilitator based in Charlotte, North Carolina, highlights how innovative practices can catalyze high-quality teaching and learning:

> We designed a curriculum based on Startup Weekend that is being adapted for use by schools in an after-school program or a one-week (five-day) day camp. We worked with Carolina Friends School in Durham to test-drive the curriculum in action through a summer program focused on twelve- to eighteen-year-olds. The students were able to learn entrepreneurial strategies, meet local start-up founders, tour businesses and hub networks, and, in true Startup Weekend manner, pitch ideas, develop teams, validate concepts, interview customers, and pitch their final MVP [minimum viable product] and concept to guest judges. Every student and teacher associated with the program left it with a completely new paradigm about student-led innovation.

Wouldn't it be cool if this crucible of innovation was not just restricted to a summer program? Parker is now working with several schools and school leaders from around the world to make that a reality.

Innovation without Action Is Not Innovation

Innovation is putting new ideas into practice.—Sir Ken Robinson

Another benefit for these intensively networked teachers is that they are constantly exposed to new and better ideas. A true OWL educator must be open to new ideas and courageous enough to try them; otherwise, that knowledge is wasted. Given the climate of high-stakes testing and mind-numbing scripted curricula, it appears that these traits are rare and difficult for education stakeholders to put into practice.

The simple fact that most classrooms today look eerily like they did a hundred years ago underscores the need for reinvention and true innovation. As the XQ Institute's "Rethink" video so eloquently points out, many of our schools have "remained frozen in time."[15] The workplace and its needs have changed drastically, technology has advanced by leaps and bounds, and the world's problems have evolved in scope and complexity. Educators can and should be at the forefront of transforming this sluggish institution into a nimble system that reflects reality in the world outside of school. They do this by possessing an unrelentingly innovative, Open Way mindset where change is embraced and celebrated rather than avoided at all costs.

Tom Skrtic, Williamson Family Distinguished Professor of Special Education at the University of Kansas, has long argued that current bureaucratic school organizational structures and the specialized professional culture of schools prevent reform, innovation, and progress toward excellent and equitable education, especially for special needs children.[16] He offers what is called an "adhocratic" structure that stresses collaboration and active problem-solving and maintains that the best solutions to the problems in education come not from administrators but from teachers and their students.

Lisa Bloom, professor in the School of Teaching and Learning at Western Carolina University, was able to put this approach into action in the 1990s using a Department of Education grant. She and her colleagues established advisory boards made up of public school students and used seed money to allow groups of teachers to work collaboratively with the students to generate solutions to the predicaments their students identified.[17] In other words, if you want innovation to flourish, give teachers the time to drive it and the autonomy to implement it!

Cultivating Innovative Teachers

> What I try to get people to understand is that how we teach the curriculum, often, is the innovation.—George Couros, author of *The Innovator's Mindset*

Leaders hoping to instill a culture of innovation will need to set aside ample time for real collaboration and open sharing, where teachers can dedicate the time and energy needed to reflect and plan. This is not an option! Encouraging teachers to individually and collectively reflect on their practice and share ideas for improvement should be as essential for a school as for its students. After alloting time, structure reflective activities and protocols that cultivate this habit—it can kickstart many teachers to innovate as never before. Educators reflecting on student learning will naturally gravitate away from didactic, outdated methods and want to explore and experiment with student-centered pedagogy. Therefore, the leaders facilitating this process need to be open to its results by encouraging experimentation and modeling a growth mindset characterized by a "failing forward" attitude. When the leaders of the school become less risk averse and shift toward growth mindsets, teachers and students will follow suit.

Setting the expectation that educators in a school are regularly reflecting on their practice, then sharing and learning from each other so they can implement improved practices, will set the wheels in motion toward an innovative

OWL culture. The network of schools implementing OWL will spawn innovative change agents who repeatedly challenge the status quo so that students can be prepared for the world as it is, not as it was.

Cultivating Innovative Students

Teaching students to regurgitate trivia about different subject areas does not inspire innovation. Getting them to create new solutions to problems and exercise their imaginations in engaging projects is much more effective. Tony Wagner, a senior research fellow at the Learning Policy Institute, discusses this at length in his book *Creating Innovators*, in which he emphasizes the need for schools that promote the skills to thrive in an ever-changing, global marketplace. He highlights various schools renowned for producing innovators, many of whose approaches converge (this will be a point of focus later in the book). Most of them focus on project-based work that gives students opportunities to flex their creative muscles through engaging, real-world applications that require interaction with experts from outside the school. Moreover, requiring students to seek connections outside the school to enhance their project work can also yield excellent results.[18] When students recruit their own mentors, the relevance of their work is amplified. They will also extend their professional networks, which may prove useful after graduation.

Open Way Learning relies on teachers willing to pilot nontraditional methods that help students develop these skills. As a result, positive sustained outcomes will happen more frequently because it's no longer just one or two adults who innovate, either because of their title or the care they bring to their work, but an entire group of passionate educators modeling innovation daily. Chapter 5 discusses research-based approaches that have shown promise in building such a culture of innovation. The Open Way Learning Academy framework in chapter 6 unpacks those methods and shows how they can complement each other.

Starting the Engines

> Working with culture is difficult; you never know what the effect of what you do will be, or if there will be a long-term effect. Structure, on the other hand, is easy: first we do this, then that, and finally this.—Jakob Østergaard, training manager at Herning Gymnasium (high school) in Denmark

At this point, you may be thinking, "This all sounds intriguing, but how can I get the ball rolling in my own sphere of influence?" Motivation is a peculiar thing. In Daniel Pink's bestseller, *Drive*, Pink turns conventional motivational wisdom on its head by stating—with research to back it up—that incentivizing with "carrots" and punishing with "sticks" are management strategies of a bygone era. Indeed, school reform is a highly creative pursuit that will not be pioneered by those motivated by extrinsic rewards (those whom Pink calls Type X), but instead by those who are motivated by more immaterial targets (those whom Pink calls Type I). Pink's primary message about them is that they are energized by *autonomy, mastery,* and *purpose.* Because of this, it is essential that leaders do not coerce subordinates into the Open Way Learning framework. Incentivizing teachers or students with extrinsic rewards or punishing them for noncompliance is doomed to backfire in the long term.

Remember Jim Whitehurst's point about one of the characteristics of the open organization from chapter 1: slow decisions mean fast results. Unlike most changes that are top-down, requiring considerable time to "build buy-in" and get everyone to comply, building an OWL culture requires a different approach. A more potent method is to plant the seeds described in this chapter to create a copacetic environment for OWL to grow organically, keeping autonomy, mastery, and purpose in mind. Providing teachers with the autonomy to make decisions about student learning through collaborative, decentralized leadership is essential. Establishing an environment of total transparency (sans hidden agendas) and trusting teacher judgment through the implementation of their suggestions will kickstart the motivation engines. This strategy can also filter down to students by seeking their feedback and designing learning experiences around their ideas and interests. As students and teachers begin to exercise more autonomy, their sense of ownership and engagement will blossom.

Once autonomy is flourishing, the pursuit of mastery naturally follows as the tasks become more personally meaningful. Refocusing student and teacher efforts toward mastery is an integral piece of implementing OWL. Anyone who thinks they are doing "well enough" will never be driven to take advantage of the free knowledge available to them. Frequent reminders of the merits of mastery could inspire others to continue pushing beyond their comfort zones to expand their knowledge and skills. The pursuit of mastery is implicitly innovative and often collaborative. Streamlining old processes, learning from failures, and improving methods are all stepping-stones en route to mastery.

Finally, reflecting on the purpose of Open Way Learning can fuel staff and students when encountering challenges. There are always reasons to turn back from the doubt-laden path of change. OWL implies a deep commitment to change and improvement, so doubts will inevitably arise for the bold souls who embark on this journey. However, to spur them on, remind all stakeholders that OWL done well can shift the trajectory of students' lives. Indeed, this

THE OWL SEEDS CHECKLIST

Use this checklist to ensure that you have integrated the cultural principles of OWL in your school's organization or network:

COLLABORATION

- Is there a functional professional learning community in place using one of the credible models mentioned in this chapter?
- Do teachers have time and space for coplanning and peer observations?
- Are teachers empowered to make collective decisions quickly in the best interests of the students?
- Are teachers and students free of undue pressure related to high-stakes tests that leads to unhealthy competition?
- Are teacher evaluations based on a wide variety of criteria so that tests aren't overly emphasized and collaboration is viewed as essential?
- Are interschool rivalries kept in check so that teachers can freely collaborate with peers in the same district, network, or region?
- Is mutual trust omnipresent in the organization's atmosphere?
- Does the school have a clear and shared vision that is consistent with the actions seen in the school on a daily basis?
- Does the school have a disposition toward a distributed leadership model?

FREE KNOWLEDGE

- Are teachers openly sharing their resources with each other?
- Do teachers regularly use resources from other teachers outside the school?
- Does the organization have a web presence that allows other educators to benefit from the resources and methods created there?
- Have teachers shifted their focus from information dispensaries to learning guides who curate resources and validate student knowledge?

INNOVATIVE MINDSETS

- Are experimentation, risk-taking, and failing forward encouraged regularly?
- Do teachers have sufficient time and structured activities to reflect on their practice?
- Are teachers, students, and administrators constantly looking for ways to improve their methods?
- Do teachers have the flexibility to pilot new approaches, even if they don't work as well as they had hoped?
- Do teaching practices cultivate innovative, outside-the-box thinking in students?
- Are teachers encouraged to share their own practices, while also retrofitting other teachers' methods and resources to fit their classroom?

pedagogy implemented en masse could also lead to a more open, accepting, optimistic, innovative, empathetic, sustainable, creative, humble, brilliant, and prosperous planet. Judging by some of the alums of schools that embrace an Open Way Learning framework, these lofty ideals can truly be realized.

The following chapters dig into the details of collaboration, free knowledge, and innovative mindsets while exploring case studies from around the world that exemplify OWL's best practices and impressive results.

3

Constant Collaboration

The smartness we need is collective. We need cities that work differently. We need industrial sectors that work differently. We need value change and supply change that are managed from the beginning until the end to purely produce social, ecological and economic well-being. That is the concept of intelligence we need, and it will never be achieved by a handful of smart individuals.—Peter Senge

Picture each of the following four scenarios:

Scenario 1 takes place within an "innovative" classroom somewhere in America. Thirty-two chairs are aligned neatly in rows with students staring at "digital worksheets" on their Chromebooks. The teacher is proud of his deft use of technology to "personalize" the student experience by having them answer cleverly adaptive multiple-choice questions after watching a YouTube video lecture (which was actually supposed to be done as homework in this "flipped" classroom). The teacher walks around ensuring that students aren't sharing answers but are understanding the content. Other than the teacher occasionally offering hints as he circulates the room, few words are spoken. The other students do not hear that conversation, however, because their earbuds are blocking any outside sound.

The teacher has "gamified" the process by allowing students to ring a bell if they get ten questions correct in a row. This is celebrated on the computer screen by a dancing bug waving a congratulatory flag. The group of students who consistently ring the bell add their own twist to the game, racing each other to see who can ring it the most times before the block is over. Another group of students, the ones who rarely if ever ring the bell, languish in an oblivion of abstract questions they don't understand. They do learn enough patterns in the questions the algorithm provides that they can make minimum progress. If students are asked why they are completing the questions, the general response is to "get a good grade on next week's test."

Scenario 2 is somewhere in San Jose, California, in a tech company office building with an open floor plan. A programmer is working with a team of twenty colleagues on a small coding project to create an app to help companies monitor and reduce their carbon footprint. The team collectively defines goals and discusses any issues either in person or on Slack and Loomio.

Following marketing research, they launch an initial product and provide customer service by sharing the responsibility of answering customer questions and making virtual site visits. They continually improve their product based on this customer feedback and use the data to develop an impressive presentation they use to formally pitch their product to a group of local venture capitalists, who agree to make a significant investment in the start-up.

The third scenario involves a group of community organizers in rural Nebraska working with migrant farm workers. They are busy unifying these workers to challenge a corporate farm that has not been paying them consistently. The organizers spend months speaking to members of the migrant communities and connecting with families to build the trust and support needed to assert their rights. They use social media to invite people to town hall meetings where, with the help of local translators and paralegals, they inform workers of their rights under U.S. law.

Eventually, they convince a law firm in Lincoln to represent the workers pro bono and sue the farm's owner. The owner agrees to a settlement before trial that restores fair pay and other benefits to the workers. The organizers then draft a bill and meet with members of the Unicameral so that future migrant workers can be protected from similar unfair practices.

In the final scenario, a young couple in Charleston, West Virginia, is trying to start a new business. The woman recently moved to the area from Ohio with her young daughter, and the man is the son of a coal mining family looking for a better life outside the small town south of Charleston where he grew up. They met at a local community college, where he is studying culinary arts, and she just started a program focused on the hospitality industry. They both work part-time jobs, and while they struggle to make ends meet, they have just signed a lease for an apartment they are going to share.

Their goal, as soon as he gets his certificate next month, is to open a gourmet chocolate shop in downtown Charleston. They recently met with someone at the Small Business Development Center, and while she was very helpful, they both left the meeting feeling a bit overwhelmed.

They both did OK in high school but still find the legal process required for this venture to be rather daunting. Nevertheless, they research online what is needed to complete the initial paperwork for a small business loan using the money he has been saving from his job at a local bakery for startup funds. They are both excited and very nervous about completing this work before their upcoming appointment with a potential lender. Each has secret doubts, but both exhibit external optimism that, with a couple of lucky breaks, they can make their dream a reality.

All four of these scenarios are hypothetical, but they are based on real events. The first scenario is deemed a "best practice" in preparing students for academic success. But does that quiet, orderly, "highly effective" class-room prepare students adequately for the real-life situations represented by the last three scenarios—thriving in a gig economy, solving real community problems, and capturing the proverbial American Dream?

There are thousands of similar scenarios that highlight how skills and knowledge beyond basic academic literacy are now an integral element of our modern society. Even so, our students are largely being taught in a manner that is antiquated. The methods are well intended but are sapping the joy and wonder of learning our children should be experiencing in every class, every day.

Students are being taught to compete with one another, to work on abstract and irrelevant tasks, to worry about their own work, and then to stay quiet and compliant. Too many American graduates then spend years painfully learning skills such as collaboration that are in high demand yet are still largely absent in many of our schools.[1]

FLATTENING THE HIERARCHY

There is a leadership theory that's been around since the mid-1800s that states "great men" are highly influential because of their inherent leadership char-acteristics, including charisma, intelligence, and wisdom. This "great man" theory assumes that leaders are born and not made and that such leaders will arise when there is need for them.[2] This idea, to a large extent, underpins the perceived value of a traditional hierarchical organization, where everyone is subordinate to a single person or small group of leaders uniquely qualified to manage decisions.

This arrangement still dominates many entities in society and is the domi-nant model within public K–12 education in the United States. Time has long past for this to change. While it is certainly a more familiar model, provid-ing a sense of control, security, and perceived ease of decision-making and follow through, it does not take full advantage of the skills and knowledge of frontline team members, fails to quickly respond and navigate through dynamic change, and reinforces an "I know best," one-size-fits-all "factory" approach to the complex task of educating young people.

> Bureaucratic solutions to problems of practice will always fail because effective teaching is not routine, students are not passive, and questions of practice are not simple, predictable, or standardized. Consequently, instructional decisions cannot be formulated on high then packaged and handed down to teachers.—Linda Darling-Hammond, Charles E. Ducommun Professor of Education, Emeritus, at the Stanford Graduate School of Education

Warren Bennis, the late futurist, professor, and coauthor of *The Temporary Society: What Is Happening to Business and Family Life in America under the Impact of Accelerating Change*, predicted that successful organizations of the future would become "adhocracies," with flexible, adaptable, and informal structures as opposed to top-down bureaucracies. His assertion was that hierarchical methods were fine for maintaining a bureaucracy but grossly inefficient in tapping into the creativity of the organization as a whole. Without loosening this "command and control" culture, the theory went, corporations (his focus as a business school professor) would stifle innovation and, in doing so, begin the slow march to irrelevance. He argued that to counter this, organizations need to establish open lines of communication, use consensus-based decision-making, and balance the needs of the corporation with those of the individual.

The point here is not that all hierarchies are bad. They may indeed be an appropriate model in many contexts. But they are not the best model for education.

Linda Lambert, professor emeritus from California State University, East Bay, argues in "How to Build Leadership Capacity" that successful, long-term change does not come by simply creating individual leaders but instead from harnessing the "energy and commitment" of a school's staff and community. Adopting a collaborative approach that leverages the talent of the entire organization instead of only a few titled leaders helps ensure that positive change will be sustained after such leaders leave.[3]

This, unfortunately, is not a common practice in the education landscape. After a strong leader leaves, most schools simply revert back to old practices and routines in place before that leader arrived. The institutionalized inertia is simply too strong without a more holistic, collaborative leadership approach that can lock the change into a school's culture. Rather than encumber the flow of information to make quick decisions, a culture of trusting collaboration taps into an organization's collective capacity to make good decisions—decisions that exceed what any single person or small group of people can provide—no matter how "great" they are.

THE LONELY TEACHER

Time for a bold statement: you might be a good educator in isolation, but you will never be an excellent one. All the way back in 1966, Seymour Sarason and his colleagues characterized teaching as a "lonely" profession in their book, *Psychology in Community Settings: Clinical, Educational, Vocational, Social Aspects.*[4] In 1975, Dan Lortie's famous book, *Schoolteacher: A Sociological Study*, stated that the teacher's work is primarily done in isolation rather than through professional collaboration with peers.[5] Has much changed?

For far too long, many educators have assumed that they can be highly effective while working in relative isolation.[6] This misguided mindset fails to tap into the vast knowledge freely available to help us improve as educators—knowledge rooted in the crucibles of student learning: our classrooms.

Jemelleh Coes, a former Georgia Teacher of the Year, reflected on the isolation she felt during her first year teaching:

> The first three months of my teaching career were miserable. I had great lessons, engaging activities, and an excellent classroom climate. Students loved being there. Yet, I spent most days crying. I had so many new and exciting ideas to

COLLABORATION AS NORM IN INDUSTRY

While Ben experienced a number of culture shocks when moving from industry to education, one of the most dramatic was the absence of peer-to-peer collaboration. In contrast to an industry culture where generating an idea by oneself was seen as taboo, in education settings many teachers would typically close their doors and only speak to each other in the hallway, at lunch, or in the teacher's lounge (and often these conversations quickly devolved into toxic complaining). The following example highlights the level of collaboration typical in his career as an engineer:

> I recall a time when I was a first-year engineer working on a problem at a manufacturing facility in Camden, South Carolina, when I learned that a colleague was working on a similar problem at our sister facility in Uentrop, Germany. By the end of the following week, I was in Uentrop collaborating with this other engineer on ways we could solve this problem for both facilities. After we solved the problem, we took the solution to other facilities in Tennessee and Delaware that also had similar operations and could benefit from our findings. This was one of countless examples of how collaboration between peers was seen as an essential element in our ability to innovate and continually improve.

share, but it didn't seem that anyone was interested in that. Even more, I wanted to learn about what was going on in the classrooms of my colleagues, and no one seemed interested in that either. I had never experienced such loneliness and disconnectedness with other adults in my life, even though there were eleven other adults on the same hall. A month later, a colleague rescued me. We began to collaborate and learn from each other. Not long after, other teachers joined in the collaboration as well. That process changed my life and my entire outlook on what the possibilities of teaching could be.

In their latest book, *Machine, Platform, Crowd: Harnessing Our Digital Future*, Erik Brynjolfsson and Andrew McAfee illustrate how emergent technologies, new products, and crowdsourced ideas are reshaping the world and how that reality must be a key consideration for leaders across every sector. Brynjolfsson and McAfee take an optimistic view by asserting that we can harness this new wave of technology and shared knowledge to improve the world in which we live. They argue that we can leverage these tools and the entrepreneurial power of the crowd to catalyze positive change. This is exactly the kind of collective action required for an open-source approach to education.

Imagine if schools were to embrace this same type of collaborative culture. Teachers could begin by simply walking across the hall to chat with a peer during their mutual planning period. Better yet, they could schedule a time to watch a peer teach and then have a nonevaluative follow-up conversation about what was seen. The easy path of creating a one-room schoolhouse within a larger school by closing one's doors and working in isolation, must be a thing of the past. Coes's example demonstrates how destructive an environment that fails to recognize the power of the crowd can be for teachers and their ability to provide rich and meaningful experiences for their students.

INEFFECTIVE PROFESSIONAL DEVELOPMENT

Regardless of your feelings toward the now-famous 2015 report from The New Teacher Project (TNTP) titled *The Mirage*, performance outcomes don't appear to be improving commensurately with the massive investment made each year in teacher training.[7] This has very little to do with teacher quality. Rather, it speaks to the general quality of professional development (PD) opportunities—or the lack thereof.

One of the primary recommendations from the TNTP report is that to improve the effectiveness of PD investments, school districts should redefine professional learning communities (PLCs). Likewise, the 2014 report from the Bill and Melinda Gates Foundation, *Teachers Know Best: Teachers' Views on Professional Development*, found that many teacher PD offerings were irrelevant, ineffective, or not connected to the core work of helping students learn.[8]

Many of the teachers interviewed for this study indicated that the professional learning they receive should be more relevant and personalized and should be provided by peers with similar experiences. This conclusion was also verified by an extensive survey conducted in the fall of 2017 in North Carolina by Hope Street Group's Teacher Voice Network. In addition to surveying 7,563 teachers, the study included seventy-nine in-person focus groups with 358 participants from across the state. The results indicated that while traditional participation-based professional development requires less time and offers networking opportunities, it also may be less relevant to teacher needs, can lack classroom applicability, and can be less engaging than competency-based professional development or professional learning.

One efficient solution to the problem of one-size-fits-all training, whose value is primarily to check a box for continuing education unit (CEU) credits, could be to encourage teachers to work together more often in the same school. However, based on results from three different surveys, it appears that teachers are rarely collaborating or visiting other classrooms.

In a 2012 MetLife survey of teachers, the majority of survey participants said that time to collaborate with other teachers had either remained the same or decreased compared to the year before.[9] According to data from the 2013 OECD *Teaching and Learning International Survey*, 54 percent of U.S. teachers say they never teach jointly as a team in the same class, compared with 42 percent of teachers internationally.[10] In addition, a full 50 percent of U.S. teachers said they never observed other teachers' classes or provided feedback.

One might expect the evidence to be more encouraging among beginning teachers, where collaboration and feedback would seem most needed. Unfortunately, it's not. In their 2007 research titled "On Their Own and Presumed Expert: New Teachers' Experience with Their Colleagues," Susan M. Kardos and Susan Moore Johnson found that, despite efforts such as formal mentorship programs, many novice teachers still work in a solitary atmosphere.[11]

Wait a minute. Don't most schools have a department, school, or district professional learning community (or, as it's sometimes called, a professional learning network, common planning team, and so forth) already in place? Yes. Though the PLC is now ubiquitous in schools and should provide an antidote to teacher isolation, too many of them are dysfunctional.

Many of these networks are "in name only," according to Joellen Killion, senior advisor at Learning Forward. What is missing is what Brianna Crowley, education and training manager for the Pennsylvania School Board Association, described as a "vibrant, ever-changing group of connections to which teachers go to both share and learn." Unfortunately, many PLCs are viewed as extra work or add-ons to an already significant workload of teaching and planning lessons.

Even the most dedicated teacher or administrator will not be able to provide a personalized, high-quality teaching and learning environment relying only on a weekly or monthly meeting with peers, regardless of its effectiveness. Even worse, when not held to lofty standards of effectiveness, PLCs can devolve into gripe sessions about everything that is wrong. Rather than identifying, customizing, and scaling effective instructional practices across a community of learners, they can codify what's easiest and most convenient, thus perpetuating a scripted, one-size-fits-all, "teach to the middle" approach.

We can do better. Of the hundreds of education stakeholders interviewed and surveyed for this book, none were unwilling to collaborate with their peers. They all clearly saw the value of collaboration but could also articulate real barriers: lack of administrative support, lack of time in the regular schedule, and lack of value by otherwise well-meaning peers. Furthermore, because many were not familiar with formal collaboration protocols that ensure time is spent efficiently, they were generally unsure of how to create a better culture for collaboration in their schools or departments. Even teachers in schools with reasonably functional PLCs were frustrated with the lack of true, professional dialogue and the tendency for the PLCs to be used as a "check box" activity to satisfy an administrative requirement.

All of this points to a chronic lack of collaboration keeping our schools from maximizing their true potential. Excellent practices are emerging in isolated classrooms but are not being scaled in the ways they could be if a collaborative culture were embraced by more educators in more schools. Relying on participative problem-solving and decision-making at a cultural level, supported by enabling technologies, good data analysis, and strong administrative support, schools can and do make better, more effective decisions in response to the needs of their learning community. This perfectly sums up why collaboration is the first, nonnegotiable element of an Open Way Learning environment. The next section provides some concrete ways to address this problem with tried-and-true solutions.

Mutual benefit is key to collaboration. If you approach a conversation ready to give it your best, to help your collaborator solve their problems, then you will both get much more out of the conversation. Over time, you will become known as a good collaborator, a great person to talk to and to help.

Remember that your cocollaborator might pay it forward rather than paying it back. Generosity is the key to both your reputation and your ability to really gain the most from collaboration. So take the time to get on the right page. Part of that, of course, is understanding what your collaborator really needs, so you can address it. Don't be afraid to ask, and to try to help them refine those needs. If you're collaborating together, make sure you share the same goal; at least 90 percent of disagreements I see between professionals stem from the two sides having different goals in the collaboration.—Allen Blue, cofounder of LinkedIn

COLLABORATION IN THE CLASSROOM

One of the best ways to witness "light bulbs" going off for students in their learning is to create opportunities for collaboration. This is not "group work" or some watered-down collaboration force-fit into a teacher-centered classroom or adult-centered school. This is free, open, and organic collaboration among students. It's messy, it's loud, it's chaotic, and it's beautiful. In such an environment, students are constantly working together in an atmosphere where, as Sir Ken Robinson says, working together is no longer considered cheating but is seen as an essential part of the problem-solving, innovation, and creating process.

Simply telling students to collaborate, especially if they have never really had the opportunity to do so other than through canned group-work activities, will likely be unsuccessful. Students need to unlearn bad habits and be scaffolded with guided practice so they see the value of collaboration. This includes best practices such as team roles, setting individual and group expectations, and monitoring progress. It is even more effective when blended with academic content through the collaboration of one or more teachers, thus giving students a much better appreciation of the real-world applications for each individual topic. This also helps keep the learning from being reduced to abstract concepts that have little or no relevance to students' lives.

Research supports other obvious benefits for collaboration apart from helping students developing a critical skill that will serve them in their careers. As far back as 1992, James Klein and Doris Pridemore compared students working cooperatively and individually and found that the former reported greater satisfaction than those who worked alone.[12] Cornell University's Center for Teaching Innovation has also done a good job of offering a succinct listing of the positive impacts of student collaboration, as well as methods teachers can use to enhance collaboration within their classrooms.[13]

Not all collaboration is created equal, however. Collaboration in the Open Way Learning classroom is more intense than in a typical school. In fact, collaboration should be part of almost every activity a student undertakes! This can take many forms, but a few of the most effective and promising are outlined in table 3.1.

Table 3.1. Pedagogical Components of Open Way Learning

	Approach	Open Way Learning version
Project-based learning	An approach where students work collaboratively to create a final product that addresses a Driving Question. Students learn content through the project, rather than before the project, then present to a public audience.	Students maintain public profiles of their work in the form of blogs, websites, social media campaigns, or e-portfolios. Assessments can relate to the real-world effect of a project or the size of the audience.
Peer tutoring	A best practice where students help each other learn a topic by teaching one another, rather than relying heavily on the teacher. The teacher can arrange pairings that will maximize the potency of this approach.	Only give students the highest level of mastery if they have taught someone else a concept in a high-quality way, thus incentivizing collaboration. Also require students to ensure that everyone in the class understands a concept before leaving the room.
Mentorships	Helping students build solid relationships with community members who are willing to assist students with academic content or life skills.	Make it a requirement for students to recruit mentors for every project they work on so they can learn to collaborate beyond the school walls and expand their networks. Teachers leverage their own networks to help students find suitable mentors, then ensure that they are maintaining relationships with mentors who could become members of the business advisory council for the school.
Field trips	An age-old method to help students see how a body of knowledge looks in the real world. These trips can create excellent engagement and opportunities for experiential learning.	Get students outside the school as much as possible. Go show them the relevance of everything they are studying and introduce them to experts and potential mentors in their field of interest. Bringing speakers in via videoconferencing tools to extend learning beyond the school walls virtually is another excellent practice.

	Approach	Open Way Learning version
Competency-based education	An approach where students master learning objectives and are able to move on when they are ready, rather than by meeting seat-time requirements.	Have students prove learning objectives together, assist each other, and present to each other. Connect students with open education resources that can help them master objectives. Have students document their knowledge on e-portfolios, websites, or blogs that can have a public impact.
Makerspaces	Spaces in schools that provide a venue for students to create art, woodworking projects, electrical engineering projects, media, 3-D printing and more.	The makerspace is central to every project and is woven into the school model rather than being used for canned lessons. Students collaborate daily to create high-quality products with real-world applicability.
Real-world connection	Assignments are clearly connected to the real world, as opposed to learning abstract concepts with little application.	Have students collaborate with experts and professionals who are applying the concepts in their careers to solve authentic problems. These people can be anywhere in the world. Assessments emphasize authentic impacts, just like a job would.
Authentic assessment	An assessment framework where students are measured on how well they can perform skills and demonstrate knowledge with real-world relevance	Students are presented with a real-world, authentic, and often ill-structured problem that requires them to draw from the "scaffolding" they have done—that is, the activities they use to increase their knowledge of a topic. They then collaborate to demonstrate that they have mastered the content in question by solving the problem, then justifying key points and steps along the way, including transfer and synthesis of knowledge to other applications.

This table shows how Open Way Learning uses highly collaborative instructional practices.

Every education stakeholder, especially teachers, will need to reframe their traditional roles to ensure a healthy foundation for collaborative student learning to thrive. In the Open Way Learning framework, the teacher's role shifts from master of content to project manager, from "teacher" to "learning guide." Teachers viewing themselves as information dispensaries will soon find themselves obsolete in the age of the Googling smartphone—if they haven't already. Students have no trouble finding answers to questions with lightning speed, so pretending to have all the answers will not impress them.

Nevertheless, even though students have become experts at accessing information, they still require assistance making sense of it and discerning which sources are reliable. Tony Wagner calls this "accessing and analyzing information" in his famous book, *The Global Achievement Gap*, which describes the critical "survival skills" any student will need to thrive in the global smarketplace (including, not surprisingly, collaboration across networks).

With countless media outlets and websites vying for our children's attention, they can easily find confirmation of any intrinsic bias and therefore need learning-guide interventions to ensure the validity of the information. Teachers become "gatekeepers" of their content area to assess the depth and accuracy of student knowledge. Accessing knowledge is only the first part of the equation, however.

Learning guides also have to become information "spelunking guides" for student explorations, guiding them deeper than they'd go on their own. The framing of a question may sometimes be the most important part of a student's successful search for knowledge. Cultivating inquiry and curiosity in students thus becomes a priority. Simple answers have far less currency in an OWL classroom because superficial knowledge is so readily available. Questioning, synthesis, and profound understanding—skills employers desire—become the new learning targets.

A teacher's role in an OWL classroom is to set up the parameters and structures for students to effectively collaborate, then to get out of the way. Collaboration isn't intuitive for students after years of traditional schooling, so setting them up to learn from their failures is essential. Providing team contract templates, pacing milestones, conflict resolution and failure analysis protocols, and opportunities for feedback and reflection are a few strategies to set students up for success. Helping students learn how to break down a large project into bite-size pieces and to keep group members accountable will become a part of the teacher's job description. Collaboration also requires a teacher to empower students and community members to be experts rather than holding onto that role. This can be uncomfortable initially, but after a while it creates a self-supporting learning community that is exceptionally productive. In short, the culture of collaboration is self-sustaining.

BUILDING NETWORKS

One of the first and most important things any teacher should do is to connect their classroom and school with the outside world. Most teachers already do a good job of this through Twitter or other social media platforms, as noted in chapter 1, but there is still room for improvement. Are you routinely bringing outside experts into your classroom in person and virtually using Skype, Zoom, appear.in, and the like? Are these experts outside traditional fields that we, as educators, tend to focus on? Do these experts interact with students in ways other than a traditional "show and tell" format?

Another good starting point is to create a business advisory council (BAC). Inviting local professionals to discuss what's happening at a school and creating venues for them to interact with students builds relationships that are mutually beneficial. This could be done in classrooms, in departments, or between teachers from across a building.

An uncomplicated way to start a BAC is to have your school join the local Chamber of Commerce. Why, you might ask, would a school want to join the

MEDIA MAKERS

Adam has leveraged his network in his Media Makers class, where students run the public relations arm of the school. He designed the class to embody the OWL approach. At the beginning of the year, he invited speakers, either in person or via Skype, to talk to students about effective messaging. Students couldn't help but become intrigued when, on the second day of class, a jovial public relations professional for a multinational corporation based in Belgium Skyped in to give them tips on how to run effective social media campaigns. They were equally enthralled by the professional photographer who demonstrated the power of lighting to change the mood of a photo using iPhones and white sheets of paper placed strategically around a model's face.

Based on professional input, the students then developed a campaign strategy and cycled through a variety of roles that helped them learn digital media skills experientially by creating content for the school's website, social media channels, and blogs. Later, Adam allowed students to choose their own roles based on their passions.

An added benefit of the class was that students proactively helped tell their school's story and pushed forward an accurate narrative that minimized the impact of gossip and misinformation in the community. As Eric Sheninger and Trish Rubin's book *BrandED* emphasizes, in a time when public education is increasingly under scrutiny, maintaining a positive public profile—the school's brand, so to speak—is becoming even more necessary.

Chamber? Why wouldn't you want to be connected to a local organization that has a mission to foster, nurture, and promote economic prosperity for the community? The school's students, even kindergarten students, are going to eventually contribute to this mission, so why not begin that interaction now?

When students and members of the school's staff routinely interact with local business leaders, nonprofits, government officials, artists, community volunteers, and the like, they get a much clearer picture of how the proverbial "real world" really works! Other clear benefits of a BAC include having a ready set of local experts who can help teachers make stronger connections and applications to various curricular topics, an authentic audience for students to highlight their work (an essential component of any solid project-based learning program), and even the possibility for targeted funding of school initiatives that are consistent with an organization's mission.

In short, every new professional you meet face-to-face or through virtual networks is a potential mentor or tutor for students. One of your primary roles as an OWL practitioner is to find ways to fit them into the school's schedule and invite them to share their expertise with more students! When you do this, you act as a bridge between your school and the outside world—a world the students will eventually need to negotiate. You'll also inevitably find ways to connect the curriculum to real-world activities the students care about.

TEACHER COLLABORATION WORKS: STORIES FROM THE FIELD

> When a teacher needs information or advice about how to do her job more effectively, she goes to other teachers. Further, when the relationships among teachers in a school are characterized by high trust and frequent interaction . . . student achievement scores improve.—Carrie Leana, from *The Missing Link in School Reform*

Though it seems that teachers would naturally share insights with their colleagues next door, it appears that is a relatively rare occurrence. Nevertheless, there are still many bright spots that offer instructive lessons about the value of collaboration.

Susan Hitt, a secondary English and language arts lead teacher at New Hanover County Public Schools in Wilmington, North Carolina, describes an instance in which her supervisor, the assistant superintendent of instruction, had everyone on the instructional team identify one focus point that year to improve instruction. It was to be an undercurrent of the work they did with students, something they would come back to week after week. While many of her colleagues selected things like reflection, feedback, and positivity, she immediately identified her one thing to be collaboration, with a goal of bringing more collaborative opportunities to high school English teachers across the district.

Hitt says, "From my vantage point on the instructional team, I could see all the amazing things each school's English department was doing, but they were very much like their own island. One school had no idea what the other school was doing."

She used technology to begin the process of enhancing collaboration opportunities for teachers across the district. She first created a high school English hashtag that district teachers who were already on Twitter could use to highlight what they were doing in their classrooms. She then created a blog as a platform for English teachers to regularly share their unique and impactful strategies and activities with their colleagues.

In the following weeks, Hitt observed an uptick in the dialogue teachers were having with each other. More important, however, was the feedback her peers provided indicating they felt more empowered and less isolated now that they had platforms to share ideas with each other. She also points out that these changes took time and that the collaboration was never forced. "It has to be organic, and all involved need to be willing to showcase their confidence as well as their insecurities. But once the doors are thrown open and educators are ready to not just share but to also listen, the path towards genuine collaboration has been paved and it will surely lead somewhere amazing."

Reflecting on this experience, Hitt remarked that "collaboration among educators should be as commonplace as that sought-after morning jolt of caffeine to kick off the workday."

Who would have thought that something as simple as a hashtag and a blog could create so much opportunity for teachers to improve their practices? With social media at their fingertips, teachers can share their work immediately with a wide audience.

Amberlee Ellett, a secondary special education and theater teacher at Mountain Heights Academy, an online charter school in West Jordan, Utah, describes her school's unique collaborative environment:

> Collaboration is not only encouraged at our school, it is essential to the success of the school. Teachers are continually sharing best practices, cross-curricular material and activities. Some of the ways that you can work toward making this successful is to establish the culture of sharing and collaboration and make it the norm, rather than the exception. We also take the competition out of the equation and allow people to explore and share in the areas where they have knowledge and expertise. We have found that by bringing it back to the benefit of the whole, rather than the individual, we are much more successful. You have to be invested more outside of yourself and have a validated experience of your work being received and appreciated.

Manes Pierre, an ELA teacher from the Holyoke Public Schools district in Massachusetts, provides this example of how peer-to-peer collaboration led to a stepwise improvement in professional learning:

> Last year, my district introduced what was called "Holyoke University," a program where educators lead the training for their peers. It was a great paradigm shift! There was a sudden increase in interest and attendance in collaborative, professional development offerings. No longer are big consulting firms simply given large amounts of money to present ideas that do not fit the needs of the teachers or students in the district. A teacher-led model of collaborative, peer-to-peer learning has created a stronger sense of trust, community, dignity, and respect to all stakeholders.

Here is an example of collaboration that impacted an entire state. The North Carolina Action Research Network, a group of teachers from across North Carolina, participated in collaborative action research projects that led not only to improved instructional practices in classrooms across the state but also to the development of a network of teachers who continue to share ideas and resources, often without meeting one another face-to-face. One participant described it this way: "I believe I am more responsive to the needs of my students and I know that I am more accessible to both my students and their parents/guardians. I think that the experience was very meaningful, and I felt like I was actually valued as an educator outside my classroom for the first time in thirty years."

The program was set up by the North Carolina Department of Public Instruction (NCDPI) and included regional coaches that were available to provide feedback to teachers on a monthly basis, either face-to-face or online. There were also two statewide conferences at which teachers could share the results of their action research. LeeAnn Segalla, an educator effectiveness leader with NCDPI, describes the network: "Many teachers were so inspired with the network that they volunteered to coach other teachers in their own schools the following year. The network's teachers were from all parts of the state and their deep level of mutual respect for one another led to true engagement in each other's work. The authenticity of the research and the rigor of the project seemed to be at the heart of the professional culture that transpired."

Nathan Strenge, a high school math teacher from St. Paul, Minnesota, describes how his team of teachers achieved remarkable results through collaboration:

> When I started teaching math at an urban charter high school, we had very little structure in place for how our classrooms should operate. [However, we] had

the advantage of a professional learning community that met for eighty minutes every other day. Both advantages were in direct contradiction to other schools I had taught in.

At the charter school, we would get students from over forty different middle schools across the city; thus, the variation in content readiness was a massive problem. But we worked as a collective team to devise a system that would help us meet the needs of all our students. Using individualized programming, technology, and intentional feedback to build relationships, we saw almost immediate returns in student growth and proficiency. In a two-year span, we moved from roughly the fiftieth percentile on the statewide math exam to the ninety-ninth percentile.

We also witnessed a culture change with teachers developing a stronger, more trusting relationship with students. The reasons for our success stem from not only having the empowered freedom to creatively solve our unique problem, but the time to collaborate was deemed such an essential ingredient to the school's mission that it was built into our schedule.

Each of these anecdotes exemplifies the immense capacity of collaboration to solve seemingly insurmountable issues in schools, districts, and state education systems. Each example highlights a different piece of the collaborative puzzle, including how things like distributed leadership, effective professional learning communities, and leveraging technology can create and sustain virtual support networks among peers. The small sampling of stories shows that in spite of a tendency toward isolation in the classroom, collaboration is indeed possible and happening in all kinds of schools. As exciting as these examples of open collaboration are, the next example is still all too common. A nationally recognized, award-winning veteran teacher from a school in the Southwest explains:

When I first started teaching we had teacher work days where teachers were left alone to plan and collaborate as they needed. . . . It was often during these times I would seek out other teachers to collaborate on lesson plans, talk philosophy, and share ideas regarding students we shared to get insights so I might reach them better. Unfortunately, now our work days are filled with mandated meetings of questionable value. Most of my colleagues are frustrated with these teacher work days and how they are structured and managed by others.

The district is actively pushing an effort that could foster more collegial collaboration—what our district administrators describe as a "distributed leadership model." But it is not true distributed leadership. Despite thinking they are empowering teachers through things like PLCs or teacher committees, the reality is that the way they are structured and run, teachers remain generally voiceless on all but a select few topics. Despite solution-oriented teacher input on various issues, we remain largely ignored.

Collaboration is undeniably the lifeblood for Open Way Learning to work. Rich, intentional, and meaningful collaboration is needed between all members of the learning community: student to student, teacher to student, teacher to teacher, teacher to administrator, administrator to administrator, administrator to off-site management, and so on and so forth. Faculty become the primary drivers of a culture of collaboration and unabashed networkers who view every professional in their local and international community as a potential educator and collaborator. The OWL faculty member thinks continuously about how to leverage the network for the benefit of students.

The rest of this chapter is devoted to providing ideas and methods for building this collaborative culture within your own sphere of influence. Even if you are only able to initiate some of these ideas in one classroom or with just a handful of like-minded peers, that's a start. As Stephen Covey emphasized, keep the end in mind and work under the assumption that as you model collaborative excellence on your OWL journey, others will notice and want to do the same. While a holistic approach accelerates the benefits of an open-source ethos at a school, the key is to start somewhere.

OPTIMIZING PROFESSIONAL
LEARNING COMMUNITIES (PLC)

What if instead of stressed-out administrators, the most frequent visitors to a teacher's classroom were supportive colleagues who used formal protocols to gather information rather than evaluate (such as those advocated by the School Reform Initiative)? This practice can start by revamping a professional learning community to follow norms articulated in the Learning Forward Standards for Professional Learning.

As more PLCs form and more research supports their impact on schools and student learning, they have become almost ubiquitous in most schools and districts across the country.[14] Judith Warren Little and Milbrey McLaughlin reported in 1993 the potential impact that the pool of collective experience in a PLC could have on equipping teachers with novel approaches and feedback for improvement.[15]

Even the most conventional principal should see the value of such a network and recognize that value by creating the time, space, and clarity of purpose so that teachers can meet on a regular basis. PLCs can discuss problems of practice, student issues, interdisciplinary initiatives, and much more—all with clear norms that ensure solution-focused conversation. Though the acronym PLC may induce eye-rolling in many educators who have wasted a lot of time in a dysfunctional one, a good PLC can be the foundation for Open Way

Learning to flourish and even offer a significant enhancement to the dreaded teacher evaluation.[16]

Beth Oswald, a teacher in the Evansville Community School District in Wisconsin and former Wisconsin Teacher of the Year, explains how PLCs best exemplify a culture of collaboration in her district and the typical challenges they face. Her story underscores the need for supportive administrators who structure schedules, budgets, and environments to promote this practice. According to Oswald,

> [Those in the PLC] have worked hard to establish a deep level of trust, honesty, and the willingness of everyone to do their part. That has resulted in a very high value for the PLC process throughout the district. These forums allow us time to collaborate on integrated, interdisciplinary lessons, units, and activities—all of which provide significantly more benefit to our students than when we have to go it alone. Unfortunately, due to recent budget cuts, we have had to cut back on the frequency of our meetings—now only meeting one day out of three. Without resources and time for training, collaboration, reflection, and revision, teachers are not likely to foster the innovative outcomes that could be possible. It's frustrating that our profession is expected to continuously do more and more with less—less time, less pay, less resources, and less respect.

As Oswald points out, without a solid PLC, many important initiatives that could greatly enhance student learning would never get off the ground. Similarly, if the teachers sense that they are not being trusted to exercise sound professional judgment and collaborative autonomy when it comes to student learning, they will inevitably offer fewer suggestions for improvement. Moreover, by being forced to use the administrator's or district's PD design (aka "Prison PD") and being subject to frequent pitches of the reform du jour, they will not use the PLC to its greatest advantage. The challenge is to be a part of the shift to ensure the PLC is living up to its true potential.

COLLABORATION AND PROFESSIONAL DEVELOPMENT

In "Is Yours a Learning Organization?" David A. Garvin, Amy C. Edmondson, and Francesca Gino offer criteria to see whether an organization is a "learning organization," a term developed by Peter Senge, senior lecturer at the MIT Sloan School of Management and author of the groundbreaking book, *The Fifth Discipline*.[17] The criteria include a supportive learning environment, concrete learning processes and practices, and leadership that reinforces learning. So while the obvious answer for any education stakeholder who was asked whether their school is a learning organization would be an emphatic yes, stop for a moment and reflect on the criteria to see if your organization is indeed a learning organization. If not, here are some steps to get there.

Just as in any profession, teachers need time and a supportive environment to make the changes to meet the growing needs of their students. Just as they provide routine, purposeful learning in their classrooms, teachers also need a similar level of such learning in order to reflect and respond to shifting educational challenges. Using the PLC to share best practices provides an ideal way to create personalized, free, professional development for teachers. By partnering new teachers with veterans or coplanning interdisciplinary units, teachers learn from each other and drive stronger teaching and learning environments for students.

Teachers can also kick their PLC up a notch by using formal protocols, such as those from the National School Reform Faculty (NSRF), Learning Forward Standards, the School Reform Initiative (SRI), or others. Such protocols and standards make these meetings significantly more efficient and intentional, giving teachers more time to reflect on their own practice and the problems facing the entire team. Including time on the PLC's standing agenda for teachers to present topics of interest they have researched provides organic, embedded professional learning. This is an incredibly efficient way to develop teachers.

Another way teachers can deepen the level of organizational trust and build stronger teaching capacity is to implement a system of "classroom rounds," a peer-observation system modeled after Japanese Lesson Study. Teachers develop a peer-observation schedule and, following an agreed-upon format and protocol, spend time in each other's classrooms watching, listening, and learning. Afterward, they provide feedback, also following a formal protocol or standard.

The schedule, frequency, and topics for the observation are always agreed upon up front, and teachers uncomfortable with such nonevaluative observations are welcome to opt out. Even if a teacher knows her entire school is not at a place to initiate a formal classroom rounds protocol, simply putting an #ObserveMe sticker on her door will get the ball rolling![18]

Tri-County Early College employs such a peer-observation system in which teachers have been formally trained to provide "Critical Friends" feedback per the NSRF protocols. The peer-to-peer observation feedback is shared as part of the standing agenda in weekly common planning meetings (also called Critical Friends meetings) by offering constructive criticism in the form of "I like" and "I wonder" statements.

The meeting also includes a facilitated discussion of a predetermined topic of common interest regarding a current issue, methodology, or trend in education, as well as time to plan for school-wide events and the next projects.

Because all of these items are discussed in a format of open sharing, continuous improvement, and consensus decision-making, the team has been able to tackle thorny issues and build a deep level of trust between peers, which also avoids problems that would otherwise lead to watercooler griping.

Another strategy for establishing a powerful collaboration model is to become part of a formal or informal network. One such example at the school or district level is Public Impact's Opportunity Culture, where schools develop systems to extend the reach of excellent teachers and principals to far more of their colleagues and, in turn, more students.[19] The model takes full advantage of the power of collaboration and has an impressive track record.

Likewise, a teacher-to-teacher collaborative model called Pockets of Excellence was recently piloted over two years in Western North Carolina.[20] Teachers from one district partnered with teachers from outside their district to create professional development goals that they then used to help each other grow and improve. This collaborative effort was codeveloped by Ben, along with David Strahan, a professor at Western Carolina University. The organic, teacher-led sharing is a low-cost form of PD and creates trust and relationships between schools that can be leveraged to improve teaching practices across an entire region. With the help of Constructive Learning Design and Hope Street Group, this work is now being expanded into North Georgia through the Southern Appalachian Learning Collaborative, which will empower teachers in formalized, teacher-led professional development and peer coaching.

The options above emphasize the power of peer collaboration and networks that can be developed and sustained over a long period. Another example of collaboration that embodies the very spirit of the "code talks" is the EdCamp. EdCamps are free "unconferences," where the participants set the agenda the day of the event and then "vote with their feet" by attending only the sessions they want to see and hear. They take organic, peer-led professional learning to a new level, empowering educators to participate in or lead sessions explicitly targeted to meet their individual needs and goals.

Given the inadequacies of one-size-fits-all training for educators, is it any wonder that EdCamps have spread like wildfire across the country? Look on any Twitter chat regarding professional development and you will soon see the comment "My EdCamp experience was the best PD I've had in my teaching career." Why? Teachers are finally given agency over their learning!

Hadley Ferguson, executive director of the EdCamp Foundation, highlights their larger mission by stating that teacher agency is the path to student agency. The key, therefore, is to bring the essential components of an EdCamp model into one's school by creating an environment where peer collaboration is the norm, not the exception, and where the best ideas, not the ones generated by the people with the most important titles, spark action. Furthermore, the EdCamp model crowdsources ideas in the same way that open information sites like Wikipedia crowdsource knowledge from all over the world. In a time of hyperconnectivity and in an environment where anyone anywhere can voice an opinion, people demand more choice and voice in decisions that affect how they do their work. This freedom to assert more control over one's destiny adds distinct value to the work and better aligns people with the purpose that led them to become educators in the first place.

For references that speak to the intersection between collaboration, professional learning and development, and an Open Way mindset, visit openwaylearning.org.

SHARED VISION AND LEADERSHIP

The Achilles' heel of distributed collaborative leadership is the chaos that can ensue when members of a team are not on the same page. Without a shared vision, these practices won't ever reach their potential. Ted Fujimoto regularly works with teacher teams and school designers to distill their school's central design principles. The intensive process forces teams to think through the end goals, how to get there, and how to sustain them over the long haul. This process is essential for open-source models because of the crowdsourced nature of their operations.

Jim Stephens, experience designer at the CUBE school in Denver and design manager for 2Revolutions, provides an example of the power of a clear mission. Stephens states that when he first started at the Denver School of Science and Technology in 2006 as a founding faculty member, their vision for equity in education was crystal clear—with clarity being the key word:

> I define clarity as the ability to see through messes and contradictions to a future that others might not be able to see. This was the first time in a school setting that I was surrounded by an entire group of people who shared a vision around equity. In my previous experiences, I was usually the only one with this vision or had maybe one other colleague who shared it. Now, since we were a start-up, we didn't have a play book, only a vision. This was so important because it meant that the vision would guide the work but there was a culture of experimentation in how we would achieve the vision and no ironclad rules. With a shared vision we could just ask ourselves of everything that we did: "Is this furthering the vision we have set forth?"

A true shared vision enables an organization's work to be less about bureaucratic rules, procedures, and habits of the past and more about an ongoing conversion that turns individual and organizational knowledge into value. An authentic, shared vision allows everyone on the team to clearly identify where they currently are on the path to the vision and specifically what they must do as an individual or in small or large groups to better achieve that vision.

In short, a good vision elicits aligned, collective action. It is at this point that empowered action, rather than top-down mandates or micromanagement, transforms the organization into a force and the vision achieves greater potency, with increased clarity and enthusiasm for the work. This is also the point when the shared vision is manifested in personal subvisions that establish aligned goals and purpose—when every decision is made as an embodiment of the vision through open communication and collaboration.

Unlike the typical vision posted on the wall—rarely referenced or updated, especially with input from all members of the organization—the constant reinforcement of a living and shared vision helps it become the core of an organization's culture. This creates a point of clarity throughout the entire organization and leads to a greater willingness to trust each other, take risks, exchange ideas, and work together to help each other succeed.

A shared vision is also essential for a collaborative culture because it clearly aligns the current and future state of the organization's goals. Peter Senge describes in *The Fifth Discipline* how "creative tension" emerges when a team clearly recognizes the gap between where they want to be (the shared vision) and where they are now (the current reality). To close this gap, Senge argues, organizations can either work to raise the current reality toward the vision or change the vision to be closer to current reality.

Too often there is a tendency to rationalize one's way into watering down the high standards that a good vision demands. Many schools, for example, claim to use an "empowered team" to make school-level decisions. Those that authentically engage classroom teachers and students by giving them the power to make meaningful decisions can claim a high level of legitimacy. If, however, empowerment simply means that teachers or department chairs are rubber-stamping and implementing decisions already made by others, such a vision becomes meaningless. Even worse, when the team's vision is undermined by such actions, the results don't yield a return on the group's investment.

This chapter has suggested several good ideas for building a culture of collaboration, but none can match the potency of an organization that follows a distributed leadership model based on a shared vision. The definition of a true distributed leadership model is what thought leaders in the field of social learning Etienne Wenger, Richard McDermott, and William M. Snyder define as a "community of practice" in their 2002 book, *Cultivating Communities of Practice*. This useful resource can help a team transition from a

A CASE FOR SHARED VISION AND LEADERSHIP

Jeff Milbourne, an independent education consultant, former high school physics teacher, and former senior policy advisor to Representative Michael M. Honda (CA-17 / Silicon Valley), emphasizes the benefit of a shared vision, explaining that it provides stakeholders a reference point to drive continuous improvement in a system. He stresses that for a vision to have meaning, metrics must be defined and used as a constant barometer to gauge progress toward shared goals. He cites an example from when he was a physics instructor at the North Carolina School of Science and Mathematics:

> I have always believed in using a diversity of data to inform pedagogical decisions, especially at the department/school level. So as an instructor at the NCSSM, I worked with colleagues over the course of about four years to develop a department-wide system of data collection and analysis, with the end goal of evaluating how well we were meeting our department's vision and goals. I found that having a common set of data and language helped guide our conversations in a way that sidestepped a typical faculty meeting conversation that might devolve into whining and bellyaching. Even teachers who were resistant to change were willing to listen and authentically engage with those data because the sources were a valid reference point against which we could agree and use to measure our progress. The bottom line is that it's hard to move forward when everyone has a different idea about which way is forward!

Milbourne emphasizes that distributed leadership provides a unique opportunity for teachers to gain additional perspectives through which to view educational problems. After all, education is a complex system and, depending on where you live inside that system, your perspective might illuminate certain problems at the expense of others. As he began assuming leadership positions at his former school, Milbourne was forced to think about problems through the lens of an administrator. He quickly learned that administrative constraints, often the result of regulation, district-wide policies, or other factors out of an administrators' control, can render good classroom solutions moot. He adds,

> It's no one's fault, just the result of the complex system that is education. That realization, however, gave me empathy for my administrative team while also helping me think about better solutions for schoolwide problems. If you've only ever lived in your own classroom as a teacher, you may lack that perspective that comes with having leadership opportunities. So while our system was by no means perfect, I did feel that our faculty members had an increased sense of agency and autonomy. Most faculty members had opportunities like I did to serve in a leadership capacity for the school and that raised our expectations of each other. The administrative support team created distributed leadership roles, which played to our strengths and would use our input and influence to improve school policy.

He also makes it clear that for such a model to work there must be authenticity, invitation, and opportunity: "Teachers must have the opportunity to serve, an invitation to serve, and an expectation that their service will have an impact."

stagnant or developing organization, characterized by seemingly unaligned habits and activities, to one that cultivates and nurtures a passion for the work they do—in other words, one that is becoming a "community of practice."

A "community of practice" is defined by Wenger, McDermott, and Snyder as a group of people who share a concern or passion for something they do and then learn how to do it better as they interact regularly. As they write: "Because communities of practice are voluntary, what makes them successful over time is their ability to generate enough excitement, relevance, and value to attract and engage members. Although many factors, such as management support or an urgent problem, can inspire a community, nothing can substitute for this sense of aliveness." Compare any of the current or desired collaborative teams or organizations in which you participate to this statement. Now think of the creative tension between that current state and the vision of your community of practice. This, in essence, defines the challenge your team has before it.

The Fifth Discipline and *Cultivating Communities of Practice* are not specifically written with a slant toward education. Nevertheless, for anyone embarking on an OWL approach to school governance, these two resources should be considered essential reading, ideally as a series of book studies with your entire team or network. Both are well aligned to John Dewey's philosophy of pragmatism and theories on functional psychology.

They can also serve as guides for implementing, nurturing, and sustaining an Open Way mindset within your organization. Schools are, after all, organizations of people focused on learning, exercising creative tension, and (one would hope) becoming true communities of practice, with the same social dynamics and interactions that apply anywhere.

Linda Lambert asserts in her 2002 article, "A Framework for Shared Leadership," that "our mistake has been in looking to the principal alone for instructional leadership, when instructional leadership is everyone's work. We need to develop the leadership capacity of the whole school community. Out of that changed culture will arise a new vision of professional practice linking leading and learning."[21]

This short but potent article offers a powerful argument for why a shared leadership model, one in which every member of the community is responsible for the learning and growth of every other member, should be an essential element for any school, especially a school that wants to build an OWL culture by tapping into the human potential of its community of learners. In such an environment, as Lambert so eloquently asserts, everyone has the right, responsibility, and potential to be a leader through the actions and ideas they bring to the organization. Does this sound similar to Red Hat's meritocracy environment mentioned in chapter 1?

TEACHER AND LT. COLONEL

The following comment is from a high school math teacher who also happens to be a U.S. Air Force lieutenant colonel in the Pacific Northwest, who wished to remain anonymous. He describes his experience regarding shared leadership in the military this way:

> In my military experience, leadership must be distributed because micromanagement would be impossible. Deployed craftsmen are spread over numerous countries performing tasks ranging from plumbing a cafeteria to placing concrete for aircraft parking. Leaders of a site may only be an E5 (low-ranking service member), but they assume great responsibility to accomplish the tasks and take care of other people. A commander may also be hundreds of miles away from job sites, so trusting, open sharing of information with my key leaders is a must. Ranking leaders openly talk about the next steps in career progression and promotions, and this grooming of leaders to leave and to take other jobs has led to high retention.

The problem is that there are still far too many schools operating within a closed, traditional model, where leadership is defined primarily by title and not by actions. Decisions are regularly made behind closed doors, through the hierarchical chain, and too often with only tacit input from the people working directly with students—much less with input from students themselves. It's a model that you or perhaps your grandparents might recognize and is likely the model that persists to this day in your own community's primary and secondary schools.

This model produces mission statements that trumpet how we are to prepare our students to be innovative, but, as some of the scenarios that started this chapter exemplify, the organizational structures generated by this model, in which a small group of people are expected to manage every student and all the people who teach them, impede innovation. A better model relies on a cooperating and empowered community that allows each member to bring unique skills and talents to bear on a common goal of education excellence.

Refer to the openwaylearning.org website for free tools that you and your team can download and use to create a true shared vision.

WHY HIERARCHIES STICK IN EDUCATION

So why is it that so many other professions and successful organizations have migrated to a distributed leadership model, while education, to a large extent, remains quite content to remain in a top-down model that has more in common with the early twentieth century than the early twenty-first century? Richard F. Elmore, the Gregory R. Anrig Research Professor of Educational Leadership at Harvard's Graduate School of Education, puts it this way:

> Contrary to the myth of visionary leadership that pervades American culture, most leaders in all sectors of society are creatures of the organizations they lead. Nowhere is this truer than in public education, where principals and district superintendents are recruited almost exclusively from the ranks of practice. As in the military and the church, one does not get to lead in education without being well socialized to the norms, values, predispositions, and routines of the organization one is leading.[22]

But why? Why do educators so tenaciously cling to a model that they themselves know is not ideal for our mission to prepare the next generation for success? Carla Silver is the cofounder of Leadership + Design, a Silicon Valley–based organization that works to build innovative capacity in educators so they can create the future of teaching and learning. She describes it this way:

> We are an industry that self-perpetuates due in large part to the fact that all of us have gone to school and we have a strongly ingrained mental model of what school is and has always been. Even if we hated school and it did not serve us well, we still accept it, as it has been, complete with all the assumptions—180 school days, report cards and transcripts, tests, classrooms, teachers as knowers and students as learners, bells, forty-five-minute periods, single disciplines that rarely connect. Adding to the ingrained ways of doing school, most teachers have actually never left school—ever—going from high school, to college, maybe to graduate school. They often did well in school and so they repeat what worked for them. But the problem is that these teachers are charged with designing learning experiences for students and preparing them for a world they literally know nothing about. They have absolutely no experience in any industry other than school. This, my friends, is frightening and potentially dangerous. This perpetuation of a model that no longer connects to the world of work, does little to ignite passion, and eschews collaboration is a slow and silent killer of the joy of learning.

This lack of cross-fertilization with other fields and other disciplines, right or wrong, is a reality we must come to grips with as educators responsible for preparing students to thrive in a world we may not truly understand. Let that sink in for a moment.

This is not being critical of educators, it's just being realistic about why it's so hard to expect educators to adopt a new paradigm when all we may know is one that operates on a set of values, rules, and timing (and some would argue, rightly so) different from that of other professions.

Allen Blue, cofounder and vice president of product management at LinkedIn and board member at Change.org, has been actively advising several start-ups in Silicon Valley focused on improving health and education. Previously, he sat on the Commerce Data Advisory Council, where he helped advise the U.S. Department of Commerce about its data resources. Allen has experience at the intersection of education and workforce development as a board member of the Hope Street Group, a nonprofit that focuses on bringing economic opportunity to Americans through a combination of policy and practice.

Blue thinks there are several reasons for the reluctance to try new things in education: "Education's rewards for innovation are far too small: people are going to take risks if there are rewards for doing so. Second, I'm not sure schools of education, and the subsequent experiences teaching, have enough contact with other kinds of work to bring in new ideas. In Silicon Valley, the constant recombination of ideas is key to innovation—I'm not sure teachers get enough contact with people who work very differently to be so consistently inspired."

For educators who spend their entire careers in an ecosystem that draws from predominantly one source—schools of education—and has relatively few pathways for advancement beyond the standard track from teacher to department head or teacher to administrator, it's hard to recognize there is a different and potentially better way.

At best, one could claim an "ignorance is bliss" excuse. At worst, one could make the dangerous argument that "we've always done it this way." Better to stick with what's been done before and not challenge the existing hierarchy and the support network that enables it to lumber along. Is this the reason other models do not get traction in education? It certainly doesn't help. It also doesn't help that because everyone, at some point, has spent time in the world of education, most likely as a student, everyone feels like an "expert" in how it should work.

Many of the solutions to our inwardly focused institutions are beyond the scope of this book. There are exceptions, however. Carla Silver describes a project she is helping coordinate called "Hack the City."

> Teachers are passionate about their work and about students. They genuinely want to do what is right and engaging for their pupils. They want their students to love school and be lifelong learners. It's just a matter of undoing some irrelevant practices that are so deeply ingrained and joining modern society. . . . Hope lies in the fact that in most cities and towns, there are pockets of innovation and creative businesses that are ripe for hacking.
>
> Hacking might look like buying a "hot desk" for a year at a collaborative work space like WeWork[23] or another similar organization, and sending teachers down to work, plan their lessons, grade papers, or cocreate transdisciplinary projects.

These spaces are sometimes incredibly inspiring and well-designed for collaboration—often the polar opposite of school spaces. Having teachers rub elbows with entrepreneurs or new organizations creates excitement. Both Hillbrook School in Los Gatos, California, and the Episcopal School in [Alexandria,] Virginia have relationships with WeWork that allow both teachers and students to hack into the city for both inspiration and real-world contextual learning.

Hacking also might mean helping a teacher find a summer- or semester-long internship in an innovative company as an alternative form of professional development. The goal here is not to move teachers out of education, but rather to help them make authentic connections between what and how they are teaching with experiences in the real world. These connections benefit the teachers, but more importantly benefit the students who will find renewed and inspired teachers who have a better sense of the skills and habits they will need in the future as well as the spaces and relationships that exist in the world outside of school.

This example of hacking speaks to how education can learn from the noneducation world—to add some much-needed new perspectives and approaches that offer a better way to meet the needs of our primary customer: our students. Does this mean that all organizations that operate with the Open Way Learning approach are communities of practice, operating with a shared vision and shared leadership? The short answer is yes. While they may not necessarily have all the detailed characteristics mentioned in this chapter, they will indeed meet its spirit and intent for an OWL culture to take root and thrive. This next section provides a clear mandate for how any school can move their governance model from the status quo to a new paradigm that embraces this open ethos.

TEACHER-POWERED NETWORKS

Everyone wants to talk about educational hot topics, like teacher performance and teacher retention, but it's hard to find people who will actually listen. Which is exactly what we need to do. We need to go to the experts, the source—the teachers themselves. It is vital that we create meaningful ways to give our best teachers a voice to impact school-level and district-level decisions that are happening. Not only does this create a better strategy to address challenges, it creates more buy-in and engagement, which always produce better results.—Dan Swartz, managing director of Resolve Talent Consulting

People naturally collaborate when there is a big, complex decision to make. They call in experts, consult stakeholders, and have in-depth discussions. Solving a multifaceted problem alone is totally overwhelming and will likely result in myriad problems upon implementation. A school or district can recognize the value of a decentralized decision-making framework and quicken the pace of cultivating a true OWL culture by seeking formal certification as a Teacher-Powered School. Teacher-Powered does not imply that administrators are not needed, it simply acknowledges that distributed leadership, as described in the prior section, is a much more empowering and nimble model than a top-down decision-making model.

This model encourages schools to adopt collaborative decision-making practices that leverage the perspective of teachers to make school-wide changes. Teacher-Powered Schools are characterized by various "autonomies" that teachers exercise over school decisions—including the learning program, hiring, school policies, budgets, schedules, teacher evaluation, tenure, and more.[24] Adopting these practices leads to more student-centered policies because of the direct contact students have with their teachers. This designation is also very useful for accelerating teacher-driven innovations and mimics the ethos of the open-source movement by encouraging nodes of a network (aka students and teachers) to make useful innovations that benefit the larger project.

Consistent with what Daniel Pink states in *Drive*, teachers in these schools have a stronger sense of purpose, mastery, and autonomy, leading to a greater ability to make changes schools need to respond to needs of students and the the larger community. When Adam visited Francine Delany New School (FDNS) in Asheville, North Carolina, he heard about the exceptional power this model had for motivating teachers. FDNS is completely teacher-governed and has every autonomy defined by Teacher-Powered Schools. Unsurprisingly, they haven't had a teacher job opening for five years!

Despite the name of the model and the rare examples like FDNS, most Teacher-Powered Schools still have principals. The key difference, however, is that just as teachers are accountable to their peers, the principal is also accountable to the teachers. In fact, in *Principal Leadership and School Performance: An Integration of Transformational and Instructional Leadership*, Helen M. Marks and Susan M. Printy caution that teachers, even working collectively, may not have the required leadership capacity to make the necessary teaching and learning improvements at their schools. They cite examples that demonstrate strong results when teachers and principals act as equal partners within an environment of mutual, professional respect.[25]

In such a model the principal acts under a "bridge and shield" framework, bridging gaps that can lead to greater trust, transparency, and open collaboration while shielding teachers and staff from administrative details that could hinder their effectiveness or that are incongruent with the mission and vision of the school. FDNS actually created one administrative position to manage the minutiae—such as managing contracts, bookkeeping, and other tasks with little effect on teaching and learning—that might otherwise bog down teacher decision-making processes. This framework is clearly within the purview of a Teacher-Powered School and is a foundational element of any Open Way Learning school.

Amy Junge, a former California public elementary and middle school teacher and assistant principal, has been researching Teacher-Powered Schools since 2009 and helped research and write *Trusting Teachers with School Success: What Happens When Teachers Call the Shots* (2012) with Kim Farris-Berg and Ed Dirkswager. Since the book's publication, Amy has continued to research and support Teacher-Powered Schools and currently works on the Teacher-Powered Schools Initiative, a joint project with Education Evolving and the Center for Teaching Quality. She describes some insights that have emerged from her work:

> The traditional hierarchy must change and the system must transform from the inside out. In Teacher-Powered schools teams of teachers secure collective autonomy to make final decisions on areas impacting student success. This looks different in different schools, and that is the point. Each team of teachers gets to decide how to create the best learning environment for their students and their communities. This looks different in Wisconsin than in New York City, but it can also look different in the same community because not all students learn the same way.

Junge also mentions some tips to create a solid teacher-powered framework:

> Taking time to collaboratively develop a shared purpose is essential. It is also important to hire new colleagues not just for their subject matter / teaching skills, but for how they contribute to the group and how they collaborate with others. . . . [by] building trust, processes and procedures that keep collaboration efficient and effective, and emphasize a willingness to listen. All of this creates a student-centered learning environment where teachers are leaders, are treated like professionals, and want to be at their schools.

Visit teacherpowered.org for more resources for starting conversations with your school about teacher autonomy or about being officially designated as a Teacher-Powered School.

CHANGING THE GAME

Greg Anrig points out in his 2013 book, *Beyond the Education Wars: Evidence That Collaboration Builds Effective Schools*, that when schools create a culture of intense collaboration between teachers and administrators, students benefit the most. Anrig engaged in a comprehensive analysis of existing research and case studies on schools that embraced a collaborative mindset with a strong sense of shared mission and trust; he found that such a mindset led to a highly functional team that worked together to improve teaching and learning practices for the benefit of students.

This is not the first time that research has shown a direct correlation between best practices, such as frequent observation, peer feedback, and formal coaching and mentoring, and an improved learning environment. Anrig found that these schools have more in common with high-performing teams *outside* of education that have rejected entrenched, top-down decision-making structures. He makes a clear and compelling argument that a deeply collaborative environment is essential for school reform.

COLLABORATION CHECKLIST

Use the checklist below to help begin your school's journey toward relentless collaboration:

- Does your team have a shared vision? Ask every staff member to write down what they think it is, then compare answers.
- Is every classroom emphasizing collaboration, not isolation, by instituting suggestions from this chapter?
- Has your school built its own network to help students connect beyond the classroom and see the true relevance of their work?
- Has your school distributed leadership by ensuring that teachers have the power to participate in decision-making that will impact students?
- Is your professional learning community potent and solution-oriented? If not, institute norms and standing agendas that will lead to enhanced teaching and learning.
- Have you leveraged the wisdom of teachers in your local school or district to identify professional development opportunities stemming from teacher-to-teacher partnerships?
- Are you attending EdCamps and other "unconferences" that provide customized and collaborative professional development?
- Have you thought about ways to promote collaboration through the arrangement of a classroom and layout of a school?
- Do you and your colleagues participate in virtual networks with other educators trying to solve problems similar to yours?
- Do you have a clear-eyed understanding of the obstacles to collaboration and have plans to overcome initial resistance?

At this point you may be thinking that this collaborative, teacher-powered, self-directed organizational model sounds all well and good, but who am I to change a deeply entrenched culture at my school, especially if my principal or superintendent is not on board? Simply bringing attention to the need for your local school to move from a comfortable, traditional model to one that reflects open collaboration and distributed leadership can be a daunting proposition, even if the culture outside of education has long since embraced it. Such cultural change can be a challenge for even the most passionate team of like-minded individuals, let alone for one person working alone.

So rather than assume that such cultural change will be easy or will happen in the short term, consider Greg Garner's advice. Garner, the design and computational thinking lead at the William and Ida Friday Institute for Educational Innovation, offers this insight to educators and teachers working to shift their organizations to a culture of collaboration and innovation:

> Slow. Down. Slower. Even slower. Keep slowing down. Changing culture is a marathon, not a sprint. It's great to have in mind where you want to go, but much like a construction project, it's probably going to be twice as expensive and take twice as long as you think. You are going to need to keep hammering on the same ideas over and over and over. About the time you think you can't possibly say your spiel one more time is about the time everyone else is starting to hear what you have to say.
>
> Changing to a collaborative culture is also going to involve tremendous professional and even emotional risk. You have to be vulnerable with your peers and acknowledge that everybody is going to have to give up something in exchange for something that's better: better for students, better for learning outcomes, and, hopefully, better for teachers. It will likely be slow and potentially painful. It's important to acknowledge the "cost" up front and know that you will have an implementation dip. Things will take longer at first, but that's because you're still new at this whole collaboration thing. Your old way of doing things is dying . . . if it's not already dead.

As you continue to read, you will see more examples, case studies, resources, and best practices that will help you run this cultural transformation marathon.

4

Free the Knowledge

Change is going to be continual, and today is the slowest day society will ever move.—Tony Fadell, coinventor of the iPhone and founder of Nest Labs

The next piece of the Open Way Learning puzzle is establishing, nurturing, and scaling a culture of free and transparent exchange of ideas, knowledge, and resources. If this mutual respect and trust is not in place within your team, it's time to go back to chapter 2 and lean into the things you and your peers need to do to see an OWL environment come to fruition. The free and open sharing of knowledge is another nonstarter in an environment where trust is not woven into the fabric of the organization. Open lines of communication ensure that the free and unfettered flow of information benefits everyone on the team, especially students. Granted, this may be a tall order, but the Open Way Learning ethos demands it!

There are a growing number of schools that have established such an open and trusting environment where political infighting, hidden agendas, micromanagement, and behind-the-scenes manipulation are virtually nonexistent. But an unfortunate number of counterexamples highlight the fact that this is not a trivial undertaking for schools still operating in a traditional environment that values hierarchical compliance over candid conversations based on mutual trust and respect. Here is one such example from an English and language arts teacher from the Boston area who requested anonymity:

My current school principal did not see the value of teachers sharing ideas and resources or any form of peer-to-peer collaboration and instead insisted on compliance to draconian rules that made life difficult for everyone. With the help of the union, we were finally able to confront the principal and insist that we be respected as professionals. She reluctantly stepped back and allowed us to do our jobs, although we still have a wide gulf of trust that has to be filled. But there is also hope.

Our school has historically been one of the lowest performing in Massachusetts, with 100 percent free and reduced lunch and an 80 percent population of Puerto Rican students. . . . The impact of the transient status of many students, made worse by an exodus of Puerto Rican students post–Hurricane Maria caused us all—including the principal—to take a hard look at the school's data and performance and face some tough facts.

We are now in the process of redesigning our school to meet the needs of both educators and students, and in doing so are finally discussing the multiple factors that have historically been left out of the conversation. Sometimes it takes a crisis, but when teachers are trusted and allowed to openly share ideas that lead to positive change for students, it changes the game.

This example shows that creating a culture of open communication and free sharing is hard work and should not be taken lightly. It's a natural response to feel vulnerable and threatened when sharing your work. Great teachers know that admitting to mistakes and failing in front of students is a powerful way to build a healthy foundation for trust, open dialogue, and mutual respect in a classroom. While it is a difficult practice at first, especially if you have been given the misguided advice to never admit to a mistake in front of students, it leads to a classroom environment firmly rooted in a growth mindset.

Instead of relying on structures that demand quiet acquiescence to decisions that are not in the best interest of students (and then complaining about them in the teacher's lounge), why not constructively criticize, challenge, and discuss ideas that bring better and quicker solutions to the table—solutions focused squarely on the needs of the students rather than on the needs of the adults?

The beauty of establishing collective free sharing within a school team is that it primes the pump for more innovative solutions to the problems a school faces. When every stakeholder of the team has an innate passion to disseminate ideas and resources rapidly and freely, they think both of their own growth and how their work can benefit others: how it benefits the whole and not just certain parts. This creates a better and more rewarding working environment that stands in stark contrast to the traditional silos that still exist in far too many classrooms, schools, and districts.

The following is from a nationally recognized elementary school teacher from New Jersey who explains that, even with strong examples of how the free exchange of resources works for students, the institutional inertia of the status quo is still difficult to overcome:

In my former school a teacher and I created digital lesson plans using Microsoft Excel and a process we called dropdown planning. . . . The plans included pacing guides that could be customized over whatever time was needed, but included the essential elements each teacher needed to address per state requirements. . . . We ultimately made dozens of these resources, and even after ten years, they are being freely shared throughout the district. The amount of time we saved teachers by streamlining our resource base was amazing.

Unfortunately, I'm now in a new district that has less value for free sharing of such resources. While there is strong administrative support, my teacher peers are stubbornly clinging to what they know and have done in the past and are reticent to change, especially if the idea is from a relative newcomer. Not invented here! They fail to see the potential in new ways of doing things, despite compelling evidence that it works for teachers and for students. As such, my proposal to adopt a similar approach was immediately dismissed. I've had to simply close my door and retreat with all my great ideas until I can build enough professional equity with my peers to try again.

Though this is one example, this dynamic is all too common, according to those we interviewed. Fortunately, there were bright spots as well, where teacher leaders and district leaders took the initiative to change the status quo. For instance, take the story of Jakob Østergaard, training manager and part-time teacher at Herning Gymnasium in Herning, Denmark. He shared how his school developed a deep culture for the free exchange of information—Open Way style.

Almost twenty years ago, our principal at the time insisted that a sharing culture was needed, and to get it started he asked all the teachers to choose at least one theme to share with their colleagues teaching the same subject. This caused quite an uproar among certain teachers. . . . Nevertheless, despite the protests, the effect of this expectation was ultimately seen as quite positive. While it is true that no two teachers are similar or that they can teach exactly the same way with the same effect, that was not the point of developing the culture of sharing. The point was to inspire others by what we each do and, in that regard, the change was seen as a strong success.

Over the years, we have continued to build on this initial experience and now the teaching staff, with the support of our management, insists on nurturing this culture as a core element of our school. . . . We have had several years where there were large numbers of new and relatively inexperienced teachers, and during those years we have all come to better appreciate the value of our open culture. It is now natural to talk a lot about what we do, how we do it, why and with what effect, and no teacher will refuse to help a rookie get started. But the ultimate benefit from this sharing culture has been quality control. We want a system where the best teachers spread good ideas about their craft to the entire organization. This is in stark contrast to the old culture where teaching was done in private isolation and where it was hard to see what good teaching was and what it wasn't.

These two contrasting examples point out that there are good and bad environments, just as in any profession. There are people who care deeply about the work they do for the long-term benefit of the organization or society and are ready to be ambassadors for positive change. There are also people who, because they know of no other way, will resist anything other than what they have always done and who are quite content to wait for the next person to take on the responsibility for change. There are also those who intentionally do the bare minimum and then spend half their time complaining about it.

The good news is that there are far more educators deeply passionate about their work and their profession than there are occasional "bad teachers" who have lost their spark. The examples we've highlighted illustrate that there are educators scattered across the educational landscape who are willing to make a difference, willing to collaborate and share ideas and resources with their colleagues to better prepare students for the twenty-first century. The trick is to mobilize these educators into collective action that can withstand the pressure to resort to the comfortable—the "way we've always done it." The rest of this chapter is devoted to ideas, examples, and tools to make this change possible.

ACCESSING FREE KNOWLEDGE WITH TECHNOLOGY

> Innovation will flourish if it is disintermediated: shorn of the externally imposed agendas and intermediaries that invite resistance and that de-professionalize teaching.—David Price

Recall from chapter 1 that this book is not simply about open-source technology. Nevertheless, any discussion of the open and free exchange of knowledge and information must clearly acknowledge how technology has changed how we learn in general and how we teach our students in particular. Open Way Learning is accelerated by the appropriate use of technology in schools; anything less than unfettered access to the knowledge available to them is a disservice to students.

Though technology is a hot topic at most schools, Open Way Learning occurs most readily and effectively when students are unleashed and have ready access to the tools and information they need. Unfortunately, schools tend toward heavy-handed restrictions on technology because of fears of inappropriate use. Imagine if Google used the same "punish the whole company" mentality for their employees that schools unwisely implement. "Sorry everyone, but Jimmy looked at some inappropriate websites, so we've filtered out any website that has the term 'breast' on it." Instead, treating poor Jimmy as an exception and training him in appropriate tech etiquette would ensure that the rest of the organization continues to have unimpeded access to any resource they need.

This is not to say that a "Wild West" approach where anything goes is the only alternative. Students, especially younger students, must be trained, coached, and then trusted to use the technology they have available to them appropriately, and they must be held to targeted and appropriate consequences if they abuse this trust. By giving up control and embracing a "trust, but verify" approach, schools show more respect for their students and acknowledge the expectation they bring to the table: that open access to knowledge is an essential prerequisite to true learning.

Apart from filtering systems that provide a false sense of control and safety, the lack of tools available for students can be another barrier to access. There are far too many classrooms with limited access to technology, where students must limp along until they can gain fleeting access to an overbooked computer lab or sit frustrated waiting for archaic hardware to do what they need. These technology constraints inhibit students from making full use of the cornucopia of knowledge available to them.

Nowadays, much of the most valuable content is video, so students need at least minimally updated tools to access it. Unfortunately, access to state-of-the-art tools for tasks such as video editing is out of reach for many schools. If Open Way Learning is to flourish, budget priorities must be adjusted to give students access to tools they will be expected to use in the real world.

Charlie Reisinger, author of *The Open Schoolhouse*, provides a variety of excellent examples from his district in Pennsylvania that show the power of opening technology policies while using an open-source methodology.[1] Reisinger not only used open-source software solutions, he gave students the keys to the machines by going one-to-one and allowing students to adapt them as needed. He then allowed students to become the trainers and tech support for the schools in the county by creating a student-run help desk. This was powerful on many levels. It was not only radical to trust students to be responsible with county property by letting them customize their own computers, it also gave them an authentic project-based learning environment that taught them countless new skills highly valued in the workplace. In many ways, Reisinger's work is the true embodiment of an OWL model!

Ideally, a one-to-one student to device ratio will enable all students to dive into the ocean of free knowledge. To reach this ideal, especially when faced with chronic underfunding, schools must rethink their approach and move away from an environment where everything is controlled. A good start is encouraging a vibrant "bring your own device" policy that encourages students to bring whatever device they can.

Many schools are afraid to open the proverbial can of worms on this one because they fear students will abuse the privilege by spending more time texting than learning. This fear is not totally unfounded but can be remedied with classroom management, monitoring, highly engaging pedagogy, and, most importantly, trust between students and adults. When done well, students clearly see their devices as more than just for social media and cat videos—or, worse, a chronic source of friction between them and adults. These devices become tools for increasing their depth of knowledge and thus part of a school's powerful and relevant technology mix.

Another thing to consider: What good is it for students to have their own devices if they have no Internet (or in some cases cell phone) access outside of school, or if they don't own a device that is appropriate for the learning environment expected at school? This is clearly an issue of equity but is also precisely where OWL networking can pay off.

A well-networked school can reach out to local businesses and community partners to see if students can use Wi-Fi in locations easily accessible to them throughout the school district. Informing students of these hotspots they are welcome to use will enable them to remain connected outside the school. In the absence of this option (such as in very rural areas), schools can consider giving personal hotspots to students without Internet. Leveling the playing field for all students to ensure equitable Internet access is integral to the functionality of the OWL framework.

Though these suggestions may seem financially out of reach, shifting school software systems over to open-source products can free up thousands of dollars currently being paid for sometimes subpar products. *The Open Schoolhouse* walks readers through the various open-source options that can meet these needs in any district.

LEVERAGING OPEN RESOURCES

OWL teachers can empower students to become active members of the learning network by connecting them with a multitude of free open education resources (OER). Perhaps the most famous of these resources is Khan Academy, which hosts thousands of lessons, primarily focused on STEM subjects. Though Khan Academy is moving into other subjects, math is its bread and butter. Teachers can curate lessons and push them out to students, then track student progress using analytical tools. Students can watch videos, read short lessons, and take interactive quizzes that adapt to their knowledge level and help them remediate any gaps in their learning.

Sal Khan, the founder of Khan Academy, envisions a world where learning is truly personalized by meeting every student where they are and helping them build increasingly advanced understandings. The good news is that this is but one of many OER tools available for educators (refer to openwaylearning.org for more details about how you can find the ones best suited for your situation).

Peer-to-peer sharing of information, materials, and ideas has been made infinitely easier with cloud-based technology, such as Google Apps for Education (including Google Docs), Pinterest, or even free platforms such as Curriki, BetterLesson, Share My Lesson, and OER Commons, among others.

But the type of organic sharing emphasized in this chapter—the type that is truly part of an OWL culture—is more than just technology; it is a consequence of solid, trusting relationships that have been formed in active networks of educators. The following example highlights just one way OER can make you a stronger, more effective, and more connected teacher.

OER IN ACTION

Joanna Schimizzi, a biology teacher with North Carolina Virtual Public Schools and state coordinator for the Public School Forum of North Carolina's Beginning Teacher Leadership Network, offers the following description for teachers who may be skeptical about the use of OER for their classrooms:

> For many teachers, our job includes the complex task of choosing meaningful assignments to help students reach a learning goal. . . . OER creates a wider network through which we can find, remix, and share examples of high-quality resources from other teachers in our same grade level and field of study. . . . OER are intended to bring high-quality, standard-aligned curricular materials to teachers for free and with the specific intent of encouraging teachers to modify the resources for their own student context.
>
> Instead of typing keywords (like "DNA Structure Worksheet") into an Internet search, OER platforms allow teachers to actually search by standard and then save the materials into an account for later remixing to meet the specific needs of their students. It's also easy to collaborate with other teachers on the remixes and leave reviews/feedback so that teaching becomes an inherently collaborative process of sharing ideas for improvement—not the silos we're currently operating in.

The use of OER creates an open-source mindset that helps teachers see beyond mastery as a grade on a multiple-choice assessment. When teachers collaborate to build assignments and assessments, they contribute to a much richer final product than the sum of the individual parts.

The collaboration often helps teachers imagine what "could be" instead of just what already exists when they teach a subject using canned or static resources. This constant collaboration and iteration not only pushes teachers to adopt more innovative ways of encouraging student exploration but also encourages teachers to engage with their students around OER practices. How are the students working? What improvements can I make? What other resources can I find? In short, they become better teachers because they are much more in tune with the needs of each student.

Massive open online courses (MOOCs) are another excellent resource for gaining advanced knowledge and skill sets and taking advantage of the fact that formal academic institutions no longer have a tight grip on the keys to enhancing one's knowledge and skills. Free online courses are currently available from platforms such as Coursera, EdX, FUN, FutureLearn, Miríada X, and OpenClassrooms, as well as from top universities all over the world. Many of these are released under a Creative Commons license that allows the savvy OWL teacher to remix the content not only for their own professional learning but to create more engaging content per their students' interests, using them as a tool to provide resources for core, targeted, supplemental, or remedial instruction.

A word of caution, however: though Khan Academy, CK-12, MOOCs, and the like are powerful tools to level the playing field for schools and teachers who constantly fight for access to the same high-quality resources available to the better-funded schools across town, computerized personalized learning platforms are inherently isolating. To be clear, these are powerful tools that can indeed help individualize and support student learning. They are not, however, a substitute for routine, personal interaction with a learning guide who uses feedback to facilitate a customized path of growth for each student. That is how an OWL teacher uses these tools. Rather than using technology to provide convenient, easy-to-deliver material that takes advantage of an algorithm to "personalize" a student's tasks (recall the classroom scenario at the beginning of chapter 3), an OWL teacher ups the ante by using them as part of a "just in time" mix of high-quality resources that help individual students target the specific knowledge they need.

GOOGLE APPS FOR EDUCATION (GAFE)

It's no secret that Google is taking over the world. Education is no exception! Google offers a variety of tools that make collaboration and sharing knowledge extraordinarily easy. In the classroom, OWL teachers can take advantage of many of Google's tools to facilitate the strategies described in this book.

Google Classroom is an excellent learning management system (LMS) like Moodle, Edmodo, and others. Classroom is highly intuitive and easily links with the entire Google suite. Teachers can push content out to students using Classroom and can create assignments with due dates, attachments (including videos, links, and Google Docs, Sheets, Slides, and so forth), and instructions. Students are notified of the assignments and can fill in customized templates created by the teacher. They can then turn in their work and send messages to the teacher using the platform.

THE FIREHOSE OF EDTECH

Feeling overwhelmed? It's easy to see the plethora of educational technology tools and resources and not know where to start. The Learn Platform, like Yelp or FourSquare for educational technology, can help make sense of it all.

Created by the North Carolina firm Lea(R)n, whose mission is to expand equitable access for all students to education technology that works, the platform allows users to discover tools using a filterable search engine, inquire about tools that may be helpful for their situation, and learn from other practitioners how the tool is being used. The biggest benefit, however, is that it allows users to give and receive real feedback in the form of ratings and comments—real feedback from other educators, not from the EdTech companies.

GAFE is also the easy ticket to the paperless classroom. After students turn in their assignments online, teachers can assess them using tools embedded in the platform or add-on applications such as Doctopus and Goobric and provide feedback on their assignments using comment features in Google Docs. Also, because Google's apps are built to streamline collaboration and sharing by hosting files on the Google Drive cloud storage platform, students can easily grant editing rights and collaborate in real time with their peers on the same document, presentation, drawing, form, or spreadsheet.

Essentially, Google Apps can remove the obstacles that block the flow of knowledge among students, teachers, and peers. In addition to being highly useful in the classroom, GAFE can be used effectively for teachers to co-create learning experiences, review each other's work, and organize staff documents. The central repository and real-time collaboration features are foundational for a functional OWL model.

FREEING KNOWLEDGE IN THE CLASSROOM

Up to this point in the chapter, the focus has been on system-level tools, platforms, and approaches that can help create a more open environment where the free sharing of ideas and information is a cultural norm and not the exception. The remaining part of this chapter focuses within the classroom and how it can take advantage of the Open Way. This starts by emphasizing the transformation from teacher to learning guide to enhance collaboration between students. So what does that look like in the context of freeing knowledge? The following provides multiple strategies teachers can use to answer this question.

Before pivoting to the classroom, however, it must be acknowledged that the sheer volume of information available on the Internet is overwhelming. Nevertheless, it offers limitless opportunities for students and educators who are willing to ride the wave rather than build a dam. Effective Open Way Learning hinges on the idea that the learning community is openly accessing information, creating new knowledge with it, and then sharing it. Rinse, repeat. Every day. Teachers and administrators must model this practice continuously if they hope students will buy into its enormous power. Sharing lesson plans, project ideas, successes, and struggles openly in the form of blog posts, tweets, social media posts, websites, videos, infographics, articles, and more helps scale the impact of effective educational practices. Meanwhile, encouraging students to do the same creates astounding engagement that can empower them to become self-actualized innovators who have discovered the joy of learning for themselves.

STUDENTS AS CREATORS

Perhaps the most important insight OWL brings to the classroom is a shift in expectations about what students should be doing. The knowledge landscape has been leveled, but many educators continue to hold onto an all-too-familiar belief that students should primarily be consumers of knowledge. OWL demands a different posture.

An OWL teacher views students primarily as creators and contributors, not as consumers. The beauty of the technological tools (including smart phones) and social networks that dominate our students' attention is that they can facilitate the process of knowledge exchange so readily. Why would we kid ourselves to think that these tools, so ubiquitous as part of our society, are a hindrance to learning instead of a resource that can make learning more relevant, personal, and powerful? Indeed, Lisa Hervey, an expert on EdTech and professor at North Carolina State University, calls smartphones "weapons of mass instruction."

An OWL practitioner will help students learn to use such tools appropriately to access and analyze the information they need and then to publish their work in creative, compelling ways. For instance, students can maintain blogs, e-portfolios, and websites that contain their best work. They could even run social media campaigns for a cause they are trying to promote. One benefit with this approach is that as they begin to publish and build an audience, their motivation will snowball and the artificial coercive incentives to spur learning used in the traditional classroom (grades, rules, and so on) will fade into irrelevance.

Even the most traditional educator will acknowledge that higher engagement leads to a greater depth of knowledge, as well as fewer discipline issues. An OWL classroom, if nothing else, is about leveraging the tools we have at our disposal to drive for the highest student engagement possible. Tri-County Early College routinely invites parents, educators, and policy makers to arrive unannounced, walk into any classroom, and see whether 100 percent of the students are engaged 100 percent of the time. As lofty as this goal sounds, it's actually an expectation for all the teachers at TCEC because of the way they have structured the approaches, activities, and tools they use each day.[2]

Another approach to drive student engagement to new heights is project-based learning (PBL). Entire books are devoted to the practice, and a growing number of educators are beginning to implement it in their classrooms. The practice involves creating a driving question that guides groups of students to a final product they will share with a public audience.

The difference between project-based learning and "doing projects" is that students learn content through the path of answering the driving question in a way that meets the established goals and objectives of the project, rather than learning the content and then "applying" it to a project at the end, as in the traditional method.[3] Many studies have demonstrated the effectiveness of this pedagogy when implemented well (note that when it is not done well, PBL can be miseducative).[4]

The Buck Institute for Education offers what many call the gold standard of in-depth training and resources for educators wishing to get started or deepen their understanding of PBL.[5] Tri-County Early College used the Buck model to develop its school-wide PBL approach. Other organizations, including Getting Smart and the UK-based Engaged Learning, also do an excellent job helping teachers and schools embrace PBL.

Part of what makes PBL so effective is that it asks students to work on projects they care about and, in doing so, enhance their depth of knowledge through real-world application and transfer of such knowledge through the project. Another significant reason PBL is such a powerful learning approach is that students often engage with mentors outside the school and then must present their work to a public audience as part of the project's final exhibition. Students often surprise educators and the public with the depth of knowledge and passion they have for a project, which emerges from a complicated mix of aversion to humiliation (if unprepared) and excitement to share their work.

Tri-County Early College students have exemplified this trend beautifully, to the point where it is becoming harder to "up the ante" to keep them on their toes by giving them bigger, more knowledgeable audiences! In addition to the audience of more than three hundred people at the Hometown Heritage project mentioned in the opening of chapter 1, students have held mock trials in front of lawyers, created social media campaigns with more than a hundred followers, pitched business ideas in front of the entire school and business professionals, and competed or presented at various conferences around the state; the Hometown Heritage project highlights student work through the "Share Your Learning" platform. Providing a diverse audience for such projects also widens the network of student mentors and supporters for future projects.

Open Way Learning takes advantage of the public audience strategy by making it a constant presence. Students might not give their best effort for an English essay if they suspect that only a teacher will read it. Peer review may change their calculus, but maybe not. What if the student's work was published in a blog they knew would have a large audience? Would they be as willing to turn in low-quality work then? Even better—what if they knew their blog post might actually make an impact on the world? Open Way Learning unabashedly leverages this natural human tendency to enjoy positive attention for the benefit of the students and anyone who experiences their work, which is freely shared with the world.

This environment expects that teachers will become astute digital media creators and curators if they want to keep pace with their students' ever-evolving skill sets. Watching students create compelling digital media and offering them constructive criticism will naturally help teachers further refine their own development in this arena. Their own motivation will grow as they observe the real-world impact of their students' work, and they will likely feel compelled to start shouting it from the Internet's virtual rooftops!

Typical classroom management issues are rarely, if ever, a consideration in this type of OWL environment because students are so enthralled with creating their own products that will have an authentic audience. Instead of passively consuming content or being bored to death by some abstract concept that is meaningless to them, they are creating content, and their learning becomes more visible through the school's social media channels and at public exhibitions.

Clearly, this classroom approach requires a strong trust in students. Sound familiar? At first, this will feel to a traditional educator like jumping off a cliff, so pushing students to share knowledge should be tempered with quite a bit of initial support and training. Start by ensuring that every student understands the permanence of their digital profile and sees its maintenance as a priority. It is also strongly recommended that you initially act as a filter, screening all student content to avoid embarrassingly poor work from being published, and that you provide targeted feedback that builds trust and skill. This temporary quality-control check is important for their sake and your sake, as well as for the public perception of the school. Nevertheless, as skill and trust grows through a "trust but verify" approach, students are able to do peer reviews and eventually earn the keys to their own external channels of communication for their own digital publications.

WHAT'S THE STORY PROJECT

One project that highlights how students can become change agents in their community comes from Middlebury College's Bread Loaf School of English. This project was designed to connect middle and high school students from across Vermont so that they could collaborate, exchange ideas, and ultimately create a multimedia narrative to advocate for social issues that they care about. What's the Story? The Vermont Young People Social Action Team (WtS) is a program that takes advantage of Vermont's Flexible Pathways Act, passed in 2013 to encourage students and schools to begin thinking more flexibly about when, where, and how students learn and how schools provide credit for such learning.

The premise is that when students are given the freedom, tools, resources, and expertise they need to pursue their own questions and then collaborate and share ideas with peers across an entire state, they are empowered and build the capacity to create real change in their own communities. Is there any better definition of preparing students for a world that is messy, unconventional, and rather hard to predict? Below, one participant discusses his role as a creator and how sharing his work made it more poignant:

> The benefits of this system . . . are clear cut from the start. We have the independence to pursue our interests in the fashion of our choice and to do so on a timeline that we ourselves create. It also teaches life skills that one would not learn otherwise. In our school, every English class is the same: you memorize vocab, you read books and have tests on what you learned, you write the same essays over and over again. While the words change, in the end the sentiment and the learning is nothing different year after year. This is not the fault of the teachers; it is just how the system works, but here we are completing interviews, doing research, making videos, and making a difference. This class is something different and it is breaking the mold.

Try matching this level of engagement and learning with a lecture, a worksheet, or a traditional essay! This work has been so successful that the program's originators are using grants to extend it to other areas of the country, including South Carolina, Mississippi, Georgia, and Kentucky, as well as to rural areas and Native American communities in the Southwest. In Jefferson County Public Schools in Louisville, Kentucky, for example, the What's the Story? Louisville program builds on the Vermont model to empower students to tackle local challenges such as abandoned properties, addiction, and early childhood education.

NETWORK EFFECTS

Another central component for freeing knowledge in the classroom is em-powering students as experts and "knowledge nodes." Teachers who are per-ceived as being the sole proprietor of knowledge in a room will have trouble scaling that knowledge effectively to predominantly disinterested students with vastly different learning styles and abilities. If, however, teachers de-throne themselves on the first day of class and then facilitate intense student-to-student collaboration and sharing of ideas and resources, the students invariably develop a level of expertise, thus shifting the dynamic.

Teachers with this mentality are irritating for students who have been in traditional classrooms, where they have mastered the game of jumping through the minimum number of academic hoops required for the grade they seek. "Please just give me the answer!" is a common refrain in a classroom practicing this approach. Thus, an OWL practitioner must develop strong relationships and constantly explain the rationale behind this practice for it to be effective and not erode trust in the community.

Such teachers must also be willing to use these relationships to continu-ously identify each student's zone of proximal development and then help create a customized path for optimal growth, with activities and questions that keep the responsibility for learning squarely with the student. Persistence is paramount to avoid giving in to the admittedly easier approach of routine, spoon-fed, stand-and-deliver lessons or lectures.

Instead of the traditional didactic approach, OWL teachers curate and pro-vide a variety of resources, as well as one-on-one tutoring and "crumbs" for students to get started down the trail of growth. Such a process works best when students choose their topics from a "buffet" of options tailored to their own learning style, passions, and interests. In this context, teachers are the quintessential learning guides by helping students go further down their indi-vidual growth pathway in a way they could not have done alone, and certainly in a way that no one-size-fits-all approach can touch.

If the topic at hand is in the teacher's area of expertise, the teacher can greatly speed up the process of finding high-quality, appropriate resources. However, when a student asks a question outside the teacher's textbook, as is often the case with PBL topics related to student passions and the real world, the teacher must be willing to say, "I don't know, let's work on a solution together." In fact, it's not uncommon for the OWL teacher to learn from a student in such situations. This is a true student-centered environment. Here's a quick litmus test: if you walk into a classroom and see everyone working on the same activity, chances are it's not student-centered.

The process described here also works particularly well in a competency-based education (CBE) framework, where students prove mastery and move at their own pace rather than following the teacher's or district's pacing. This may challenge some educators because there may be students who finish a course in half the allotted time and others who struggle to meet minimum pacing expectations.

Nevertheless, the initial logistical hurdles of this approach also provide incredible network effects. With a class full of empowered researchers and confident content masters, there will always be a student who can help a peer with a given learning target. Astute OWL teachers are then essentially "cloning" themselves by pairing students so that these so-called experts can provide initial help and support to students who have not yet developed this same level of mastery.

We learn . . .
10% of what we read
20% of what we hear
30% of what we see
50% of what we both hear and see
70% of what is discussed
80% of what we experience personally
95% of what we teach to someone else.
—The Learning Pyramid

Teachers can incentivize this process by withholding "high mastery" until a student articulates their knowledge by helping a peer.[6] If a student feels that they have done sufficient work to prove mastery of a specific learning target, they can do so at any time, ideally through what William Glasser, author of *The Quality School Teacher*, calls a "show and explain" authentic assessment, a one-on-one or group assessment with the teacher.[7]

If they want to go above and beyond, as some students always will, they become deputized as teacher's assistants for that specific learning target. The teacher is still the ultimate gatekeeper to ensure, via a "show and explain" assessment, that the minimum depth of knowledge for a specific learning target (standard) has been sufficiently demonstrated, justified, and, at least in a PBL context, applied.

Another advantage of the CBE framework is that there are no traditional grades—only constructive feedback and authentic, personalized assessment that enables growth. No extra credit, no participation grades, no homework grades, nothing other than high mastery, mastery, in progress, or targeted remediation. A growing number of schools are adopting a mastery transcript approach, and a significant number of colleges and universities accept this over the traditional transcript.[8]

The efficiency of this process, once it is fully operational, is astonishing. Granted, it is a lot of work to get there, but the payoff is dramatic. Having thirty students actively teaching each other, for example, far outpaces the thirty to one student to teacher ratio that beleaguers countless educators. It naturally creates a vibrant learning community that imbues the values of autonomy, compassion, and openness in students and teachers alike. This process is also the secret sauce behind the 100 percent engagement challenge mentioned earlier in this chapter!

Nevertheless, teachers can expect initial pushback if implementing this aspect of an OWL structure in their classrooms, especially if other teachers in the school are not using this approach. Students and some parents may

FREE KNOWLEDGE CHECKLIST

Use the checklist below to remove the barriers to the free exchange of knowledge and ideas in your school.

- Does your local school have an environment of mutual trust and collaboration that promotes a sharing culture?
- Does your school give students and teachers unfettered access to technology they need to be connected inside and outside school?
- Has your school investigated replacing expensive proprietary software with open-source alternatives?
- Are teachers currently using open education resources in their classrooms? Are teachers creating and sharing their OER remixes?
- Are teachers in your school using Google applications or other software to promote collaboration and sharing in the classroom and to create school documents?
- Do students create content for projects instead of simply consuming it?
- Are students encouraged to share their work on social media, blogs, and websites?
- Do students regularly tutor each other during class and view themselves as experts in the material?
- Are teachers frequently blogging, posting, or otherwise making an effort to share their work broadly to contribute to networks that help other teachers?

Add your school to the growing number involved in the "Share Your Learning" network (http://www.shareyourlearning.org).

complain that they aren't doing their job as a "teacher" because they are not teaching (at least in the traditional way they are accustomed to seeing).

The late Grant Wiggins, former president of Authentic Education in Hopewell, New Jersey, and member of the ASCD faculty, once said, "Decades of education research support the idea that by teaching less and providing more feedback, we can produce greater learning." In other words, the less "teaching," the closer you are to an OWL classroom or school, unless, of course, it's one student teaching another. Keep your eyes on the prize, however. Eventually, the newfound freedom and confidence students develop as they share their knowledge will turn the tide. This approach is also in line with a growing number of schools and networks, such as the New York Standards Consortium and the National Center for Open and Fair Testing, who are saying no to the overemphasis on traditional grades and the culture of test prep.

Just like the open-source ethos that programmers use to constantly add their own ideas, iterate with peers, and then quickly prototype the next version of the code, each member of an OWL learning community has an equal opportunity to participate and contribute from their own perspective. The shared mission of developing bodies of knowledge for a class, a project, a school-wide activity, or a district initiative are made more potent through collaboration and free exchange. Every member of the team—students to superintendents—feels compelled to contribute to the overall well-being of the learning community of which they are an integral part. It's admittedly messy, unconventional, and rather hard to predict. It's also a beautiful thing to witness.

If we don't know where things will end up, won't we risk a bunch of failing test scores? Well, after Adam shifted his classroom to this style, his scores jumped fourteen points in one year for biology and "showed growth" in his subject for the first time in five years. Indeed, teaching less created more learning! This might provide some reassurance, at least until the era of standardized testing is behind us.

SHARE YOUR RESOURCES

Clearly, the free sharing of knowledge and resources is essential to this overall framework. Now it's your turn! Visit openwaylearning.org to openly share your work and remix the work of others. Also, review the checklist below to define your next steps!

Intrepid Innovation

Know anyone who uses Ask Jeeves anymore? Compaq computers? Drives a Studebaker? Anybody still rockin' the slide rule? (Unironically?) When we sell our homes, why are we concerned with updated appliances or the removal of popcorn ceilings? Things change. Preferences change. The reality of the world our students are entering has changed and will continue to do so. The jobs of today are not the jobs of yesterday and almost certainly won't be the jobs of tomorrow. We aren't innovating for innovation's sake, we are innovating because it's a posture we must assume. We must be learners, ready to adapt to the changing environment.—Greg Garner of the Friday Institute

As the above quote so humorously illustrates, it would be totally preposterous to use those outdated products that have long lost their relevance and usefulness. It is equally ludicrous to continue with an educational approach that is out of sync with the needs of today and tomorrow. This is why a *culture of innovation* is essential for any school to remain, at minimum, relevant and, ideally, vibrant, nimble, and responsive to the needs of its community.

This chapter will attempt to demystify the concept of innovation using examples from experts within and outside of education who have lived in environments where innovation is more than just a passing fad. The examples and resources highlight that innovation is driven by a commitment to excellence through collaborative continuous improvement. This is what makes innovation—especially innovation in an open-source environment— so cogent. It is all about questioning and challenging what you did yesterday because there is a chance that it may not be what's needed to maximize value for tomorrow.

Collaboration and the free exchange of knowledge are simply not enough to establish an Open Way Learning environment at a school. Indeed, schools can just as easily collaborate and exchange ideas in ways that perpetuate rather than transform the current system.

In all likelihood, if you ask a random group of educators, most would say that their classrooms, schools, or districts are already collaborative and that they routinely engage in the free exchange of innovative ideas. This is increasing evidence that the terms "student-centered," "personalized learning," and "teacher leader" are misunderstood and clichéd buzzwords flippantly used to impersonate change and hide what's really a superficial rehash of what was there before. This chapter, however, will not discuss the watered-down versions of innovation force-fit into a traditional model; rather, we'll look at innovation rooted in the Open Way Learning ideology.

Innovation depends on and is an obvious outgrowth of the previous two characteristics of Open Way Learning. Without a deep commitment to crowd-sourced collaboration and uncompromising, transparent communication based on the free sharing of ideas and resources, innovations will be few and far between. This is not to suggest that innovation is limited to such contexts or that traditional organizations are necessarily bad. It simply means that the power of an innovating organization shouldn't be underestimated.

In fact, when an organization consciously harnesses, coalesces, and directs innovations with laser-like focus on its core mission and vision, it operates in what Mihaly Csikszentmihalyi called a state of organizational "flow."[1] This dynamic capacity can't be matched in the typical hierarchical organization, where collaboration and free sharing are discordant. A patchwork of disjointed improvements may exist, but they are rarely sustained and certainly don't have the same synthesizing power that helps the organization's mission and vision come to life through the actions of its people.

Steve Kurti, former research physicist at NAVAIR and Loma Linda University and cofounder of Innovation Academy (formerly known as Table Top Inventing), provides an example of "flow" in his experiences with schools and students all over the country during weeklong innovation camps.

Some innovations are simply impossible without openness and free sharing of ideas. If you have ever worked through the Stanford "Design Thinking" process with a group, you can observe a significant difference when the group hits a state of "flow" in the Ideation phase. Prior to "flow" ideas are on their own and sterile, and if a single person says, "Can't," "won't," "shouldn't," or any other negative judgment of an idea it immediately and severely stops the progress toward flow.

On the other hand, when all members of the group are instructed, "Anything and everything is possible for the next few minutes," the ideas flow more freely.

Openness and free sharing are not the only requirements to reach a state of flow in Ideation, but without them a group cannot reach flow. The free flow of ideas in the divergent state of thinking is an extremely fragile environment. It can be destroyed by just about any negative thought, idea, or comment.

The implication here is unmistakable. An innovating school, one that has all the pieces of the Open Way Learning model in place, is finally, truthfully, and with solid evidence producing results that align with the idealistic and almost universal school mission of preparing students for the twenty-first century. Except it is no longer idealistic. It is happening. It has the organizational potency to reject the entrenched current state and say once and for all that there is a better way—and we are doing it.

Once all three tenets of the OWL framework are in place, the learning organization employing them will begin to customize solutions to their own context and scale them quickly to every classroom. OWL then becomes the catalyst for a school that has woven the open-source mindset—Jim Whitehurst's "the Open Source Way"—into its culture at every level so that it can truly claim to be innovating all day, every day.

CULTURE OF INNOVATION

If we as a global population are going to not only survive but succeed, we need a means to quickly and efficiently assess different paths, recognizing that the best path for person A may not be the best for person B. Unless we can collectively and creatively innovate from the whole range of ideas, someone (possibly whole groups) will be left out to a destiny of loss and hopelessness. Our education systems are an essential part, if not the primary part, of this dynamic and as such, they must adapt for the new global reality that's upon us. Change can't wait!—Laura Watts, global account manager for INVISTA

Tom Vander Ark, CEO of Getting Smart, defines improvement as "doing things better" and innovation as "doing things differently to improve outcomes dramatically." His assertion is that most school reform efforts, especially at the high school level, stop at improvement. Some of these produce modest, sustainable successes, but many don't result in the impact suggested by the hype. Why? Improving means that the traditional model can remain in place—the same one that's been narrowly defining "success" for our students for well over a hundred years.

Embracing an honest approach to innovation requires rethinking everything that impacts student success and then eliminating all barriers that inhibit such success by any means necessary. We are, after all, dealing with some real problems in our schools that require innovative solutions instead of window dressing. Such innovation requires intense collaboration with transparent testing and iteration to get right.[2]

So why is true innovation not happening in more of our schools? Terry Heick, former classroom teacher and now founder and director of TeachThought, has assembled a comprehensive summary in his article "12 Barriers to Innovation in Education."[3] In it he provides an unflinching indictment of how the status quo model has cobbled together norms, policies, and approaches that, while well intended, ultimately thwart the creative, innovative thought we desperately need.

Heick cites a few examples such as one-size-fits-all lessons, scripted curriculum maps, mandated professional learning networks that are "learning" in name only, and a maze of red-tape policies that dampen any innovative thoughts that may emerge from such a stifling environment. These are things you may recognize from your own personal experience. It's time to raise our standards and expect something better!

However, just because these are *typical* elements of an educational system does not mean they are *essential* elements of an education system—especially one that is more in tune with the needs of students than it is of the needs of adults.

Larry Rosenstock, one of the founders of High Tech High, has ample insight into how true innovation in schools can change the paradigm of education altogether. He encourages educators to question the status quo when launching a new school or redesigning an existing school. Rosenstock remarks, "We want people to be perplexed—to embrace the paradox of starting new schools." In this context, he offers five precepts that are worth considering:

1. When starting a school, ignore a few basic axioms. There are a lot of things you don't need: bells, public address system, separate bathrooms [for teachers and students].
2. We should ask students to use their head, use their hands, make things, and think about things.
3. We should think more about production technology than consumption technology.
4. Keep tinkering with your local school, taking things apart and putting [them] back together. Let people mix it up, keep it interesting. Balance stability versus churning—not unstable but not stuck.
5. Let students do most of the talking and adults do most of the listening. Be about revealing, about uncovering (not just covering content), asking students to do field work, and to demonstrate their learning.

A KERNEL OF OPEN WAY INNOVATION

One of the original Open Way Learning ideas began in 2006 with the Open Source Teaching Project, when Michele Villarreal, a gifted education teacher in Murfreesboro, Tennessee, was able to put her students in contact with academics, business leaders, policy makers, and thought leaders from around the world through a program that helped students make real-life connections to academic content.

The program was run by the nonprofit Sage Leadership Partners and involved interviews with experts in a wide range of fields. The interviews were then posted online, free for anyone to access, accompanied by teacher resources, including lesson plans and blogs. According to the project's website, over sixty-five people were interviewed, including Nobel laureates, MacArthur "genius award" fellows, Guggenheim fellows, scholars, a United Nations ambassador, a Pulitzer Prize–winning journalist, and more.

The good news is that the Open Way Learning model presents a way to embrace these and other game-changing ideas, plus offers a powerful antidote to traditional barriers to innovation. On the other hand, we will never implement such ideas or remove such barriers through inaction. Problems are solved by trying something, assessing how it went, and then revising and trying again and again. In other words, they are solved by building a culture of innovation through action, as Sir Ken Robinson states in *Creative Schools: The Grassroots Revolution That's Transforming Education*: "Innovation is putting new ideas into practice."

> Today knowledge is ubiquitous, constantly changing, growing exponentially. . . . Today knowledge is free. It's like air, it's like water. It's become a commodity. . . . There's no competitive advantage today in knowing more than the person next to you. The world doesn't care what you know. What the world cares about is what you can do with what you know.—Tony Wagner, author of *Creating Innovators*

Clayton Christensen, the Kim B. Clark Professor of Business Administration at the Harvard Business School, asserts in *The Innovator's DNA* that there are five characteristics of innovative thinkers: associating, questioning, observing, networking, and experimenting. His work is based on studies of a number of innovative individuals and companies including Steve Jobs, Jeff Bezos, Paypal, and Tata Motors.

Christensen makes the case that innovators are people or organizations who synthesize ideas by connecting the dots within and outside of their current context. In that process, they are willing to fail and learn from their mistakes as they go. This means they are not constrained by the comfortable way things have always been done, where there is a greater emphasis on risk avoidance than on creative action. He is also able to provide various examples that highlight how innovation is influenced and enabled by people (for example, Google's approach to hiring), processes (for instance, Keyence sales team members observing the company's production lines), and philosophies (such as Amazon's "two pizza" teams).

Christensen's argument, like the many other examples cited in this book from outside education, provides significant insight into how teachers and administrators can build similar innovation within their own classrooms, schools, and networks. In fact, Christensen actually ends his book with a call to take these ideas to children! Who better to heed this call than educators?

Scott Anthony's *The Little Black Book of Innovation* has a clever approach of digging into the culture behind innovative organizations. In doing so, Anthony highlights key differences between the various types of innovation and offers a twenty-eight-day program showing how your organization can master the key steps of innovation. Using a "Frequently Asked Questions" format, he provides practical advice applicable to any organization wishing to build a culture of innovation. The overall message is that true innovation is deceptively simple: identify a problem and solve it through constant iteration and follow-up.

Will such an approach work in education? Absolutely! This powerful little book was the framework for a highly successful school-wide "Shark Tank" project at Tri-County Early College in 2017.[4] Students developed a MVP (Minimum Viable Product), defined a lean start-up plan based on market data they curated through research and surveys, and analyzed available resources to establish prioritization criteria for the MVP. The final products were then presented and defended—Shark Tank style—to a group of local business and community members. The PBL teams then used the "Innovation Insights" from inductees to the National Inventors Hall of Fame as the basis of their peer, self, and project reflections. Powerful stuff!

All this is well and good, but anyone who thinks they are one degree of separation from the solution to all the problems in education is clearly mistaken. No such silver-bullet solution exists, including adoption of an OWL approach. A constant focus on continuous improvement through experimentation, analysis, and iteration, however, will work.

This, in a nutshell, is why a culture of innovation has such potential to be the catalyst to clear the path to educational excellence. Whether it's through action research, the scientific method, the engineering design process, or simply old-fashioned trial and error, collaborative, open innovation is a powerful process every educator should use every day. Every class. Every lesson. Every staff meeting. Every parent conference. Every interaction. It is a potent tool for creating incremental and stepwise improvements in teaching and learning environments.

In fact, an innovative culture will become a bit neurotic because you and your team will never be able to settle for anything less than excellence. No matter how hard you try, there is always more work to do. You will never reach a "perfect solution." And that's not a bad thing.

Nathan Strenge sees the main design flaw of traditional education as a discontinuity between the nature of academics and the nature of the outside world. He remarks:

> The world around schools is changing at an ever-increasing rate. We live in an exponentially expanding world of technology and global connectedness, yet schools by design are isolated places of academic learning. If one looks up "academic," it says . . . "not of practical relevance; of only theoretical interest." The bedrock of our education system, academic learning, can be defined as having no practical relevance. This, by nature, puts all of our traditional schools at risk of not being responsive to the community they serve. . . . [Students'] lack of awareness of relevant problems creates disengagement, boredom, and worst of all, a misinformed view of the world around them. Without [an informed view], they cannot possibly be expected to address the real problems that exist now, and those that will be amplified by the explosive rate of change we are seeing.

If you believe Strenge's assertions, then shifting the methodological focus from pure academics to real-world relevance will be a primary driver for a move to a culture of innovation. This assertion is also at the core of the Open Way Learning mindset. If you don't agree, you need to come to grips with the very real possibility that the students you interact with may leave school unprepared to deal with a world that demands skills such as agility, adaptability, collaboration, critical thinking, and grit. The fact that you are this far in the book, however, means you are probably inclined to keep learning about how OWL might impact the students in your community.

KICK THE TIRES AND LIGHT THE FIRES

The initial fragility of the innovative process should not be taken lightly. Changing anything implies risk-taking, and most people are (healthily) risk averse. Thus, any disruption of the initial ideation phase can send a group of well-meaning educators or students back into their shells of normalcy and comfort.

REKINDLING THE JOY!

Eric Hennigan, a software engineer at Google and former computer science instructor at the University of California, Irvine, now works with students from across the country through innovation fellowships. Here he describes his experience teaching:

> Students are very reluctant to suggest an answer, for fear that they might be wrong, and [they] are fighting a behavioral lesson that they pick up in elementary school. Although young students often have the bravery—or lack of self-awareness—that allows them to speak up in class, it's essentially beaten out of them over time. There's nothing more degrading than being laughed at by the teacher or the rest of the class. The other children are so insecure themselves that they'll take every opportunity to pick themselves up by mocking others. Even for the talented students, if they are praised about their intelligence they will end up taking fewer risks and try fervently to be wrong less. This dynamic means that almost everyone will leave the education system less excited than when they entered. . . . Teachers then have the problem of rekindling the excitement and interest we were all born with. To accomplish this, we must find ways of fighting the earlier training: we must encourage participation and the mistakes that come with exploring.

Whatever your role in the education ecosystem, you can help define a problem at your organization and set norms that promote divergent thinking by saying, "Yes, and . . ." rather than "No" or "What if?" This is an important first step in nurturing an innovative culture. Amy Junge, the Teacher-Powered Schools director for evolving education, puts it this way: "The culture of saying yes. Allowing teachers to try things, open to failures and learning from mistakes." But what about after the brainstorm, when your team or students are attempting to implement an innovative approach? What if you . . . gulp . . . *fail*!?

Jeff Milbourne thinks the key benefit of an authentic culture of collaboration and innovation is that teachers fail with purpose and continuously improve. "At the end of the day, it comes down to mindset. When you live in a culture that promotes collaboration, you value fluidity in ideas and . . . become less dogmatic about 'what works.' You're willing to try more things and feel supported in those efforts. . . . [Y]ou're willing to fail with purpose, meaning you learn from your mistakes in a way that promotes continuous improvement."

He provides an example in which he and a small group of his colleagues at the North Carolina School of Science and Mathematics sought to overhaul the way they taught an introductory physics course that had historically been problematic for students. He describes why this team was able to collaborate and develop innovative pedagogy to improve student learning:

> I'd posit that a culture based on mutual trust and respect provided the professional foundations that gave us the confidence to be truly innovative. This sort of culture is a prerequisite for any authentic innovation in teaching and learning. Still, it takes time. In my case, I had known these colleagues for a few years and we had tried to engage with each other socially—a few beers can go a long way in helping you develop relationships with colleagues!

Milbourne also noted that this culture created a sense of accountability to the broader school community, where people weren't just being innovative for the sake of being innovative. The deep sense of trust and respect meant that each member of the team felt accountable to the other members, giving each other their best and not wanting to let anyone down. It also provided them a measure of emotional safety that made failing a welcome learning experience.

This example reinforces the assertion that candid, intentional communication is central to a culture of true innovation. Developing positive communication norms can be a struggle, especially if your organization has a history of poor communication. Still, any one person or small group of people can make a difference simply by making a visible and public commitment to change in their classroom, in their department, with their team, or at their school.

According to Alison Reynolds and David Lewis in their article "The Two Traits of the Best Problem-Solving Teams," modeling this level of generative behavior requires cognitive diversity and physiological safety, as well as a targeted investment in applicable best practices from chapters 2 and 3.[5] These approaches enable improved collaboration and free exchange of ideas—and the rest of the organization can't help but notice the contrast. Less open and transparent communication practices elsewhere become obvious, providing what is essentially a crowdsourced incentive for change. Through this process, the Open Way has affected real cultural change elsewhere in society, and it can have the same cultural impact within education.

Milbourne's emphasis on relationships should also not be underestimated. Innovation can't be mandated and will not thrive in an environment that does not feel safe and free of hurtful criticism. Rather than spending the first week of class reading the syllabus, going over a bunch of classroom rules, or, even worse, diving straight into the curriculum, teachers should invest in getting to know their students and help them see that their classroom is a safe place to share ideas, to experiment, to fail, and to keep trying.

For example, Adam, a former Outward Bound instructor, spends ample time at the beginning of each school year having his students do trust and team-building exercises and answering questions of the day that encourage them to share stories and insights with each other. In this manner, he gets to know his students better, they get to know each other and themselves better, and the level of trust that is established makes his classroom a hallmark of innovative thought for the rest of the year—far outpacing the progress that would be made if he launched into his curriculum from day one.

Ben takes a similar approach and emphasizes the ethos of his classroom environment with the following prominently displayed sign: "In this room, you are to keep an open mind, ask questions, and think for yourself. Always remember that your teacher could be wrong." These are but two examples of how teachers can build the trust and open communication needed for innovation to thrive in an OWL classroom.

School leaders can facilitate this change by getting creative about ways to promote informal collaborative partnerships, including coffee talk, their own team-building activities, and, yes, maybe even getting a beer! If relationships are strong, communication is easier. When collaborative, free, and open communication is the norm, true innovation soon follows.

POSITIVE DISRUPTION

Nobody has ever won a Nobel Prize by doing what they're told, or even by following someone else's blueprints.—Joi Ito, coauthor of *Whiplash: How to Survive Our Faster Future*

Think for a moment about some of the changes in human history that forced institutions or society to rethink the status quo. At the heart of many was a person who dared to challenge the rules and norms: Martin Luther, Susan B. Anthony, Harriet Tubman, Rosa Parks, Phoolan Devi, Lech Wałęsa, and the unknown "tank man" from Tiananmen Square.

In their 2016 book *Whiplash: How to Survive Our Faster Future*, Joi Ito and Jeffrey Howe describe a concept based on Moore's law, arguing that the number of transistors in an integrated circuit will double approximately every two years, thus fueling an exponential advance of technology in the modern world. Innovations are going from ideas to the marketplace in significantly less time each year, and crowdsourcing has completely changed how information is shared and used. Does this ring a bell?

Ito and Howe also state that breakthrough innovation rarely comes from people following the rules. Rather, it comes from a bit of disobedience: "Disobedience, especially in crucial realms like problem solving, often pays greater dividends than compliance. Innovation requires creativity, and creativity—to the great frustration of well-meaning (and not so well-meaning) managers—often requires freedom from constraints." In addition to emphasizing concepts such as discovery and experimentation that many educators should already be familiar with, they emphasize embracing failure as part of the innovation process. A healthy degree of "creative disobedience" can also encourage us to look at problems in a new, unconventional way—a perfect ingredient for an OWL environment of innovation![6]

Given that a significant amount of time and energy are spent on control and compliance in most of our schools, both for teachers and for students, it's no wonder that they are rarely examples of innovation. It doesn't have to be this way, and we can no longer afford it to be this way! The days when only an elite few have the privilege of being innovative and everyone else complies with a set of rules and procedures designed for control rather than creativity are long gone. Innovation is the paramount skill for every student in today's world. And done well, it requires a healthy dose of rule-breaking.

Thomas Kelley, the general manager for IDEO—a highly successful and award-winning international consulting and design firm founded in Palo Alto, California, in 1991—also emphasizes how rule-breaking is an essential element of innovation. In his 2001 book, *The Art of Innovation: Lessons in Creativity from IDEO, America's Leading Design Firm*, he explains that IDEO starts with the premise that everyone is, by nature, creative and then builds on that to create a culture of innovation with the hallmarks of free expression of ideas, deep collaboration, and a willingness to allow people to break a few rules as they think about things differently and challenge old assumptions.

This formula has produced phenomenal results and has led organizations all over the world to adopt IDEO's approach to design thinking to make innovation a way of life. This includes becoming part of the curriculum for Project Lead The Way (PLTW), the nonprofit organization that provides hands-on STEM activities that help students develop the in-demand knowledge and skills they need to thrive in today's global economy and offers training and support for elementary, middle, and high school teachers.

Reading Kelley's book not only will help you better understand the design thinking process but will also have a profound impact on your appreciation of why innovation is essential for any organization wishing to remain relevant in today's hyperchanging environment. Put another way, the days are over when a school can sit back, do what it has always done without seeing the need for innovation, and still expect students to show up.

Regardless of your views on school choice, there are simply too many options available to bury your head in the sand and say that what worked in the past is still good enough. Schools that fail to recognize this are on the path to mediocrity and irrelevance. On the other hand, a learning organization constantly seeks input, gauges the value it provides to the community it serves, and continuously improves itself. When something is not working, true leaders step up. Rather than seeking blame, they identify the root cause (by asking "why?" at least five times—even if it gets to a painful truth) and then work with the team to do whatever it takes to correct course.

Daniel Pink used one of Kelley's quotes in *Drive* that is applicable to this context: "The ultimate freedom for creative groups is the freedom to experiment with new ideas. Some skeptics insist that innovation is expensive. In the long run, innovation is cheap. Mediocrity is expensive—and autonomy can be the antidote." Educators would be well served to make this their attitude toward innovation and to work toward autonomy by distributing leadership in a teacher-powered, student-centered framework, as discussed earlier in the book.

EMBRACING POSITIVE DISRUPTION IN SCHOOLS

So what does positive disruption look like in a school? In the classroom, it means encouraging students to constantly think "outside the box"—and outside the textbook. They may look for you to provide them with constraints that aren't actually there so they can retreat into their comfort zones. Resist that temptation! Instead, encourage them to make up their own rules, try to be supportive of their ideas (even the outlandish ones), and, above all, avoid antagonistic interactions that reestablish an unhealthy power dynamic.

This will be difficult at first. On balance, it is likely to be counter to what you learned in the credentialing process, whether from a university, student teaching experience, or mentors. Still, staying true to this open approach will begin to create an innovative student environment. It's also important to realize that the students might not know what to do when you tell them to challenge a few rules, so you will have to bolster their confidence as they enter this new realm of creative disobedience.

For educators and leaders, creative disobedience can mean the classic "ask for forgiveness, not permission." Teachers can be bold and try out new strategies that test the normal boundaries of the school environment. New scheduling, assessments, and teaching strategies that surprise students and shake up the typical routine should become commonplace.

At Tri-County Early College, for example, new teachers are told to try their best to do nothing that looks like a traditional classroom. The key here is to be intentional, to orient yourself toward solutions, and, above all, to try something. Even if it flops, you are trying to improve, to grow, to get better. That is what spreads the innovative mindset to others. After all, you won't have to ask for forgiveness if you end up better than where you started! With enough patience and courage, that's exactly what will happen. You don't see many Nobel Prize recipients apologizing, do you?

LEARN BY DOING, FAILING, AND IMPROVING

Disruptive leadership will lead to disruptive innovation.—Eric Sheninger, author of *Uncommon Learning: Creating Schools that Work for Kids*

Innovation in an Open Way Learning environment encourages learning by doing—gaining direct experience and then using that experience to improve. It is based on flexibility, sharing, and community. Early adopters will want to start with low-stakes efforts and build complexity as they build the organization's capacity. Members of the community should be encouraged to offer ideas, but they should also feel free to add their ideas and contributions as they feel comfortable, which may require providing platforms to collect ideas from team members who are less inclined to verbalize them.

The environment should also be based on a continual and transparent review of results, experimentation, and iteration. This means that team members are regularly looking for improvement opportunities to get closer to realizing the organization's vision. Such a working atmosphere is based on the

INNOVATIVE TEACHER EVALUATIONS

Douglas Hodum, a high school science teacher and former Albert Einstein Distinguished Educator Fellow, cites an example of collaborative, open sharing that led to an innovative revamping of the district's teacher evaluation system in his district in Farmington, Maine:

> I am currently working within my school district to develop an innovative teacher evaluation system. Throughout this process, there has been open participation from all the stakeholders and the buy-in has been nearly uniform. . . . This process has been open and trusting, leading to a better solution [because it] allowed the conversations to be more transparent and informed from all vantage points.
>
> The new system includes stronger tools for teachers to collaborate on assessments, ideas for measuring student growth in our classrooms, and . . . clear and open communication between administrators and teachers. While this has happened to some degree in the past, the new system requires teachers to provide their own evidence to support their growth in their practice. This enhances the transparency and trust in a system that used to be viewed with suspicion and has shifted the emphasis to teacher growth and away from fixed mindset proficiency.
>
> The result is that teachers are no longer working in isolation. Teams of teachers are now working together to develop customized tools to measure student growth. Doing so requires the open exchange of ideas and is better enabling teachers to hone their craft.

principle of meritocracy, where ideas from any team member are reviewed by peers who provide feedback and suggestions to improve them.

Douglas Hodum's example again confirms how the comingling of collaboration and free knowledge exchange can lead to innovative approaches. His emphasis on "customized tools" highlights the need to move away from one-size-fits-all solutions to the diverse problems schools face. When teachers are trusted to create such solutions with input from administrators, students benefit and the school becomes a much more enjoyable place to work (what Daniel Pink calls "Motivation 3.0"). OWL educators also become better poised to take advantage of published research in academic journals and ideas shared from colleagues in their respective networks—their own "source code"—to remix and prototype solutions that fit their own situation and context.

Embracing the teacher-powered model, as emphasized in chapter 3, can also accelerate an innovative culture. According to Amy Junge, "In Teacher-Powered Schools teams of teachers secure collective autonomy to make final decisions on areas impacting student success. This looks different in different schools, and that is the point. Each team of teachers gets to decide how to create the best learning environment for their students and their communities."

INNOVATION THROUGH THE ENGINEERING DESIGN PROCESS

True innovation comes from a collaborative cycle of iteration, where members of the team are always bringing new ideas to bear on what has been done before. Not surprisingly, given that coding and software engineering are two fields joined at the hip, the engineering design process is the method of choice for Open Way Learning. It fuels the rapid prototyping of ideas and, when used effectively, synthesizes the collaboration and free exchange of ideas from the brainstorming stage through execution and sustainability. This, by the way, is also why teaching coding to children is so important. They build critical programming skills and then can use the "bug fixing" process to learn from failure and develop a stronger growth mindset.[7]

Although there are a number of variations on the engineering design process, including the "Plan, Do, Study, Act" model,[8] they generally involve these key steps: (1) defining the problem, (2) collecting data and information, (3) generating ideas to develop potential solutions, (4) planning and developing prototype solutions, (5) implementing and testing the best solution, and (6) using feedback to improve the solution. Rooted in the scientific method, the engineering design process is used by engineers, scientists, and researchers all over the world to formally drive the improvement process.

This methodology is versatile enough to tackle small problems as well as large, school-wide issues. Here, as an illustration, are some classroom examples:

- Define problems based on observation and research: What does each student currently know compared to what they need to know?
- Brainstorm to develop a variety of solution options: What are the best ways to address each student's individual knowledge gap?
- Develop a plan of growth and success: What specific actions are needed to relate the content to what each student cares about?
- Test and retest plans: What data and evidence is needed to determine the effectiveness of the plan—that is, what worked and what didn't?
- Iterate to continually improve: What adjustments would maximize the growth and enable the success of each student?

When done well, the engineering design process makes innovation a natural extension of a culture of collaboration and open sharing of ideas and information. Every member of the organization builds the individual and collective capability to identify and solve problems of practice by rapidly responding to their root causes.

OPEN WAY INNOVATION IN ACTION

The Open Source Pedagogy, Research + Innovation (OSPRI) project at Duke University is another example of cutting-edge work that is bringing an open-source approach to education, specifically in the area between student learning and teacher learning. This joint effort between Duke's Social Science Research Institute and their Innovation and Entrepreneurship Initiative uses open-source principles to design and scale an open education model that increases open access and learner agency, both within and outside education contexts.

Aria Chernik, founder and director of OSPRI, has helped launch numerous high-impact, student-centered open learning projects such as creating free 3-D printed custom prosthetics for amputee clients in North Carolina and Haiti, integrating open-source concepts and technology into student-developed education technology, partnering with Red Hat's CO.LAB initiative to close the gender gap in STEM fields by teaching middle school students collaboration through coding, embedding an open-by-design ethos to transform curricula across K–12 and university classrooms, and expanding access to computer science education for students underrepresented in technology fields. OSPRI also launched three new courses at Duke: Open Source Education Innovation, Foundations of an Open Source World, and Open Source Education Technology.

AN INNOVATIVE CULTURE LEADS TO BEST PRACTICES

When applied in an OWL environment, innovative teaching and learning practices such as competency-based education, problem- and project-based learning, personalized learning, and place-based service learning become more potent because they are under the constant scrutiny and reflective improvement of a collaborative team of passionate educators focused on deeper learning for everyone in their learning community. Chapter 4 introduced some of these practices in the context of enhancing a free exchange of ideas. The following section revisits them through the lens of innovation.

Project-Based Learning

The reason OWL jibes so well with PBL is because the PBL model integrates collaboration, real-world relevance, public audiences, innovative thinking, group problem-solving, and more into its structure. However, doing PBL in an OWL environment amplifies its impact because it pushes the envelope on each of these points and provides a template for scaling these effective practices. Table 3.1, for example, touches on some of the nuances of OWL-infused PBL.

PBL provides an innovative vehicle for instruction that can be adapted to any subject area in any place. It emphasizes the importance of student voice and choice, thus creating the student-centered environment required for OWL. Teachers can define starting and ending points for a project, but students must choose which path to take in order to maximize their own learning and they must address their personal goals for the project as well. Final products are open-ended, thus creating an opportunity for divergent, innovative thinking.

It's no coincidence that Tony Wagner's book *Creating Innovators* strongly endorses the PBL methodology as a suitable tactic to cultivate these attributes. Wagner spotlights High Tech High in San Diego, California, as a model school and describes the students' journeys through PBL units there. PBL is also a foundational practice for the Open Way Learning Academy model outlined later in this book because of its ability to teach students through experience the OWL tenets of collaboration, free exchange of knowledge, and innovation.

Competency-Based Education

If we want students to understand the nature of the outside world, why do we give them grades? Competency-based education (CBE) and other similar approaches such as mastery-based or personalized learning allow

KENTUCKY STUDENT VOICE TEAM

Rachel Belin, director of the statewide Prichard Committee Student Voice Team, describes an innovative campaign she coordinated with students across Kentucky. In an effort that highlights the value of intergenerational collaboration, free sharing, and innovation at scale, the Student Voice Team (SVT) helped redefine high-quality teaching and learning by initiating a series of policy conversations with over two thousand other students from across the state to improve Kentucky's schools:

> Starting in 2012, the Prichard Committee for Academic Excellence was exploring ways to include students in its work to improve Kentucky education. The students who volunteered to help were obviously new to education policy-making but were eager to collaborate and contribute to making our schools better and more inclusive of student voice and perspective.
>
> The project gave the students a unique opportunity to actively question and examine the very educational systems they had been passively participating in for their entire academic careers, solicit the feedback of their peers, and then develop tangible solutions to make the system better. Through several initiatives they designed and developed, the students found ample opportunities to amplify and elevate their own voices and those of their peers in Kentucky's education decision-making process. Specifically, they spoke at local rallies about their firsthand experiences with inadequate education funding; they authored over fifty op-eds about such pressing subjects as under-resourced schools and low academic standards, the need to integrate more students in school governance bodies, and inequities in the postsecondary transition process, many of which were published in the state's largest newspapers. They also presented at policy conferences and joined Prichard Committee staff numerous times in testifying before the state legislature on their research around the role of student feedback in bolstering school and teacher effectiveness, adding students to superintendent screening committees, and the problem of diverting funds from the state lottery away from need-based college scholarships.
>
> Using technology to foster the team's collaborative efforts, including Google Docs to remotely contribute to their collective writing, GroupMe and Slack to coordinate internal communications, and Google Hangouts and Zoom to host group strategy sessions, the team of students, which grew to include students from Kentucky's urban, suburban, and rural communities, was able to experience firsthand how policy change happens and how they could play a role in ensuring that it does.

Zachariah Sippy, an SVT member, contrasted the real work this network was engaged in with what he was supposed to be learning in his high school government class:

> It makes no sense when you consider that even in the typical social studies class, the very place where we are supposed to learn what we need to know about how government works in order to be engaged, future citizens, we learn little to nothing about how our public schools are governed. Our conversations with young people

(continued)

(continued)

> across the state reveal that even in high school government, history, and debate
> classes, most students remain in the dark in terms of their most local governance.
> As one student told us, "In school, we talk about everything, except school itself."

This innovative, grassroots effort clearly put these students firmly in the driver's seat, advocating for greater student voice and the need for serious youth and adult partnerships to improve Kentucky schools. In short, they lived government rather than just passively sitting through a class, studying irrelevant textbooks and worksheets. And while the bills the students spearheaded during various sessions in the Kentucky legislature did not all pass into law, the experience these students gained in this process will obviously serve them for a lifetime and is something no traditional approach can touch.

Belin adds an ironic twist, however: "Some of the students who were spending time meeting with lawmakers were actually disciplined for missing their classes." That succinct statement speaks as much as any example in this book about the mismatch we have allowed to develop between the real education our children could get and the education they are currently provided—one that unquestioningly follows control and obedience to the status quo instead of what is best for students.

students to move at their own pace by demonstrating mastery in a given course of study rather than sitting through a course and being graded on unnecessary assignments that reinforce something they already understand. Entire states, including New Hampshire, have adopted this approach because of its proven effectiveness.[9]

Many teachers have historically struggled with how to teach to every level in the room, so they usually end up aiming somewhere in the middle. This bores the students who are always seeking a challenge and frustrates students who have not yet fully understood the topic at hand. Instead of assuming one hundred hours of biology class will teach a child biology, CBE assumes that a child knows biology when they can demonstrate mastery to the teacher on the competencies contained in its course of study, ideally doing so via a series of performance assessments rather than arbitrarily scheduled traditional memory recall tests.[10] This shifts the classroom conversation from "What is the minimum I need to do to get (fill in the blank with the student's desired grade)?" to one that reinforces an iterative, growth mindset. It also means that students avoid being saddled with bad grades on assignments or topic tests as the rest of the class moves on, oblivious to the fact one student is lost.

Many workplaces are inherently competency-based in this way, especially those that follow a high-performance work system (HPWS) model.[11] How many workplaces say to every new employee that they cannot move to another position until serving one hundred hours in their current position? New employees are generally on-boarded and given more responsibility as they demonstrate their skills and abilities through hands-on proficiency. Time in the role may be a *component* of this process, but the primary factor is demonstrating observable skills that meet a set standard. Though there may be some exceptions such as the hundred-hour Yoga teacher certification or times when an organization needs to control rapid turnover, the normal approach is to promote people when they show they are capable. Why shouldn't schools work this way?

As alluded to in chapter 4, implementing CBE in a classroom or school will require retooling teachers' skill sets, thus creating countless invitations to innovate. Some of the approaches that emerged at Tri-County Early College when CBE was implemented include flexible scheduling, class-wide peer tutoring, alternative assessment strategies, just-in-time academic support frameworks, and a unique response-to-intervention plan. Every one of these innovations was created by a teacher-powered professional learning community (PLC) responding to the immediate needs of students.

Every adult in a school truly implementing OWL constantly creates and applies ideas to ensure that every student is successful and takes full responsibility to reach each child. This means that innovation becomes an essential everyday practice. It has to. In an OWL environment, teachers constantly collaborate, share ideas with peers, and create new and innovative solutions to address the individual needs of each student. No excuses and no shortcuts.

If you are an educator seeking the Holy Grail of "leaving no child behind," employing project-based and competency-based methodologies in an OWL approach may be the answer. When students are perpetually encouraged to collaborate, exchange ideas, and innovate, generating creative project ideas, helping a friend learn an abstract math concept, and presenting work to a public audience will become the new normal. However, students' "new normal" will make them exceptionally potent change makers in the workplace and beyond.

These are but a sampling of the countless methods (think source code) that can be tested and customized in an OWL environment to meet local needs. Each school's set of innovative practices will be different. The beautiful thing is that OWL educators will apply the design thinking process to their craft without even realizing it. In so doing, they'll methodically refine their teaching and learning strategies, based on real-time data, to address their local needs.

This is the point when teachers, students, and others are not afraid of making mistakes and are willing to fail forward or, to use another mantra from IDEO, to "fail often to succeed sooner." It's when every member of the learning community embraces the true innovation Tom Vander Ark defined earlier—not the fake innovation of simply rearranging the deck chairs on the Titanic. This is also the point at which they can proudly see an elegant and customized Open Way Learning environment take shape.

DON'T WAIT, INNOVATE!

The process of failing fast, learning fast, and driving continuous improvement is exciting for anyone, but especially for educators, given the stakes of the work with our next generation. Innovation cannot be a part-time activity, sidelined to a club or after-school program. It also can't be reserved as a reward for "gifted" children. Innovation must become the norm for *any* school, and it is unquestionably the norm in an OWL school. Making innovation an essential part of everyone's role makes a school much more nimble and responsive to the needs of students and the community and makes the school enticing to any forward-thinking educator.

This last piece of the Open Way Learning puzzle means that everyone in the organization is bringing innovations to bear on student success. Sustained

INNOVATION CHECKLIST

Use this checklist to kickstart an innovative ethos in your school.

- Would you describe your local school's culture as innovative? If not, what are the obstacles and opportunities regarding innovation in your school?
- Do teachers, students, parents, and administrators frequently brainstorm and strategize ways to continually improve the school?
- Do school faculty encourage positive disruption in student work?
- Are teachers willing to fail forward in their classrooms by experimenting, reflecting, refining, and improving?
- Are administrators encouraging the process of innovating by acknowledging the inevitability of mistakes and a fail-forward attitude?
- Do parents understand the value of this experimentation and recognize the overall aims of each new innovation? How is the school communicating the changes to parents and the community?
- Are teachers and students applying the engineering design process to their work in systematic ways that have led to legitimate improvements?
- Is the school identifying weaknesses and trying out new nontraditional but research-based teaching and learning methodologies, such as problem-based learning, competency-based learning, and the like?

positive outcomes will happen more frequently because those outcomes no longer rely on one or two adults but instead are driven by an entire group of passionate educators. An innovating school, one that has all the pieces of the OWL model in place, is indeed a force to be reckoned with. It has the organizational potency to reject the entrenched status quo and to say once and for all that there is a better way and we are doing it, so either join us or get out of our way.

OWL is not just a way to make educators more efficient and open. It is a way to overhaul an antiquated model by highlighting and scaling practices that actually work, then surgically eliminating the ones that are not working in the best interest of our students. This is easier said than done. Yet it can be done when all of the ingredients are established with fidelity and purpose. The next chapter provides actionable ideas you can use to make this happen.

6

The Open Way Learning Academy

The first step in teaching students to innovate is making sure that educators have opportunities to be innovators themselves.—Suzie Boss, author of *Bringing Innovation to School: Empowering Students to Thrive in a Changing World*

THE STUDENT'S JOURNEY

Luis still wasn't sure what to make of his new school, the Springfield Open Way Learning Academy (SOWLA). It had basically questioned everything his previous eight years of education had taught him. He was still weirded out that teachers called themselves "learning guides" and didn't "teach" the way he was used to, and their constant emphasis on collaboration annoyed him at times. Why couldn't he just work alone on something!? Sometimes he felt he had to unlearn everything that had worked for him before to get the grades he wanted. Truth be told, most days he loved it, but today he was feeling grumpy. This frosty December morning wasn't a typical day. It was exhibition night—his second one. He awkwardly fiddled with his tie to see if loosening it might allay his anxiety. It didn't.

The first exhibition night had been OK. The learning guides and his peers had given him plenty of feedback about how he could improve, so he was determined to do better tonight. This time the stakes felt higher because his mentor, a local newspaper reporter, and all the parents would be there, not to mention all the community members who would come because of the school's social media barrage!

Even worse, his group felt far more dysfunctional than the last time. The project started strong and his group generated some amazing ideas, but one group member, Taylor, made promises that she hadn't kept. Even though the group's contract had a firing process, no one held Taylor accountable, so she failed to pull her weight. This left some loose ends for the rest of the group to tie up before exhibition night.

Swimming in these unsettling thoughts, Luis hopped off the bus and walked briskly to his advisory, his daily meeting with other students interested in a similar career path. As he entered the room, Ms. Elm greeted him warmly. He tried to hide his worries, but Ms. Elm always seemed to have a BS detector. After she checked attendance and made a couple of announcements, she approached Luis. Luis reluctantly shared his concerns, though he never mentioned Taylor by name. Ms. Elm reassured him that they could have a discussion during PBL time to ensure he was ready.

Luis and the other students spent the rest of the period convening with their accountability groups, where they set goals related to school, life, and career. Luis set a goal to give feedback to Taylor, finish his data analysis, prove a math learning target, and follow up with a pediatrician he was planning to shadow the following week. Ms. Elm had students share their goals and wished them well for their upcoming presentations. Finally, Ms. Elm asked each student which skills lab they needed to attend that day.

Luis was struggling to analyze his data from a recent lab experiment conducted to test his group's greenhouse prototype, so he headed to the math learning guide, Mr. Khan, for his skills lab. He presented his data, and Mr. Khan partnered him with another student who had conducted a similar analysis the week before. Luis quickly grasped the concept after seeing the other student's process, then generated two graphs and a table of his statistics to better represent his data. After he hurriedly posted them on his blog and updated his lab report on a Google Doc shared with his groupmates, he went to Mr. Khan to prove mastery on his first statistics learning target. He was starting to feel better about the day. Two goals already met! Woohoo!

Next, he had Mr. Khan update the school's master flex schedule so that he could head to his biology class. His teacher, Ms. Greeley, had posted the question of the day on the Google Classroom site, but he had not yet had time to look at it. Their school-wide project had students create solutions for food security issues in the local community by collaborating with international organizations that had experience innovating and implementing such best practices. Ms. Greeley, along with every other teacher at the school, had been developing probing questions that required students to research and answer in a way that helped them meet the goals of the project.

Today's question of the day asked students to discuss their research on biotechnology within their groups and prepare for a short class-wide seminar on whether genetically modified foods should be used to address food security issues. Luis's group had some strong opinions and heatedly debated the merits of this technology. They had to first back up their opinions with credible sources and then negotiate a consensus before presenting their thoughts and evidence to the other members of the class.

Ms. Greeley circulated through the class, listened for quality arguments, asked open-ended questions, and checked the veracity of everyone's research. After looking at Luis's notes and hearing his well-considered contributions, she told him he was near mastery of the applicable biotechnology learning target. He just needed to clear up a couple of points so that he could firm up his mastery with her in a "show and explain" interview right after school.

Luis's confidence soared as he headed to PBL time in the SOWLA makerspace. He loved working in the spacious environment, with its natural lighting, woodworking tools, media studio, 3-D printing shop, art supplies, 3-D printers, Arduino hardware, and electrical equipment. It seemed that the creative possibilities were endless, and he was always inspired by the work he saw other students doing there.

He headed to the lounge area in the corner to meet with his teammates. Luis was determined to resolve any issues his group had before the quickly approaching exhibition night. Taylor looked sheepish today, and she avoided eye contact as Luis approached.

To address the driving question of the project, Luis's group had worked with a Peruvian non-governmental organization he was able to contact through his uncle to create a cheap, functional greenhouse prototype. The organization had experience with various greenhouse designs through the work they had done in Andean villages. The group participated in two Skype calls with the firm's community outreach contact. That was quite a logistical hurdle to get over: different languages, different time zones, technology issues . . . but they had made it work! The team was even able to get agreement to use the firm's blueprints as a starting point to build various prototypes. They could then decide how to make optimum use of their materials to make the most effective and inexpensive final design.

They had also gotten the manager of a local hardware store to donate the materials to construct their final design. Their plan was to build the final design at school and then transport it to the local food bank to help alleviate hunger in their community. Luis's family had used the pantry in the past five years as his father struggled with unemployment, so this project meant a lot to Luis. Luis's group cataloged their process on a blog and website, worked with multiple mentors locally and internationally, and created a Facebook group that had over two hundred followers.

They had some polishing to do, so Luis got busy touching base with each team member. They decided they needed to publish their blueprints on the website, practice their presentation, and fix a broken piece on their mini-prototype for their table that night. They had expected that Taylor would sit back as usual, but she shocked them by speaking up. "I fixed the broken prototype last night and made some last-minute improvements to the blueprints. They're already on the website. I didn't want to let you guys down."

Luis was stunned. After picking his jaw up off the floor, he gave Taylor a high five and shared his relief and appreciation. The group rehearsed their presentation with another group, then traded feedback using the peer feedback protocol they had been using all year.

As the first guests arrived for the exhibition, Luis couldn't wait to share his project. Hordes of people came by his table and expressed how impressed they were with his group's work. He answered questions easily and saw Taylor starting to speak up more. The newspaper reporter even interviewed him for a story they wanted to write about the project!

By the end of the night, Luis and his exhausted group members shared some enthusiastic high fives. Beaming with pride, Luis's father Roderigo gave him a tearful hug. He had never seen his reserved son speak in public, much less to hundreds of strangers, and would never forget it. After this remarkable day, Luis could hardly contain his emotions. He never knew school could feel like this.

THE TEACHER'S JOURNEY

It had already been a long morning when Amy Elm's students started trickling into her advisory. She came in early to finish up a blog post and accompanying video about a past project that she was preparing to send to a team of teachers she was working with through Teacher2Teacher. This was her third post of the year, and she was feeling more confident about getting her story into the education blogosphere. She couldn't wait to share this latest project with a wider community and was excited to send the school's link out in a Twitter chat she would be moderating that evening.

Today was a big day for SOWLA because of the upcoming exhibition night. The teachers had posted invitations in the local paper, on the radio, and through all their social media channels. The project's Facebook page already had over seven hundred likes! They had also sent personalized invitations to local politicians, school board members, and, with the help of the local

Chamber, their business advisory council. Amy knew that sharing their best practices with a public audience was a core value at SOWLA, so exhibitions were mission critical.

Nevertheless, she was feeling nervous about the event, as she always did. There were sure to be skeptics in the audience who wondered whether this type of education was as rigorous and valuable as that offered by the other, traditional district schools, or if it was just fun and games. Likewise, there were always some students who hadn't fully bought into the projects or didn't follow through on their ideas as effectively as they could have. Amy was happy to help students learn from their failures, but the public was not always so forgiving. Would one or two bobbles undermine the credibility of the school?

As Amy's students started trickling in, she greeted each one and asked them how they were progressing toward their goals. When Luis walked in, she knew something was up and made a mental note to check on him later.

One of the most valuable things about the forty-five minutes they spent each day in advisory, doing things like post–high school planning, mindfulness activities, Genius Hour, and team building, was getting to know what made each student tick. That's why she immediately knew something was up with Luis. She had implemented accountability groups in her advisory so that her students could hold each other accountable to short-term and long-term project, academic, and personal goals, as documented on their individual plans for success. Amy could see how this process helped students feel empowered to take full ownership of their education—something she had not seen in her prior school, which ran just a fifteen-minute standard homeroom class. Watching students complete goals was as exciting for her as it was for them.

Another thing she loved about her advisory was helping the students manage their internships and job shadowing activities. Amy had always enjoyed watching student motivation surge when students finally found internships that resonated with their interests. SOWLA had devoted a significant portion of the week to these internships after Mr. Bridges, the principal, had obtained a waiver from various seat-time requirements. Luis's mentor had called the previous day with a question about Luis's internship, so she was excited to update him about that during their brief conversation.

After spending a few minutes with Luis and offering him some advice on how to navigate the all-too-common group drama that befell many SOWLA students, Amy verified that other accountability groups were keeping their SMART goals up to date. Although she loved the ability to use Doctopus to provide real-time feedback to each student, she always enjoyed the one-on-one conversations better. Afterward, she updated the skills lab placement list on a Google Sheet shared with her colleagues.

At a recent Critical Friends PLC meeting, Amy and her colleagues created this document to individualize instruction for students using flexible, day-by-day scheduling. The principal had applauded the teachers' efforts and headed off concerns from parents and the central office about whether the students were getting enough face time with each of their teachers.

As her advisees exited and her skills lab students entered, Amy turned on her air traffic controller persona. She began by asking students to set a goal for the period. Because Amy was a history learning guide, her students set goals that related to history learning targets, a combination of state history standards, historical research skills, and interdisciplinary topics that students attempted to master.

Many learning targets were packaged as creative performance tasks such as art projects, debates, presentations, and mini-PBL projects that allowed students to choose their own pathways, emphasized skill acquisition, and ensured that they knew the required content. Other learning targets were reworded history standards that students could master one by one through demonstrating adequate depth of knowledge.

Amy moved around the room, checking on individual student progress by asking questions to gauge current depth of knowledge based on the mastery criteria rubrics she had established for each learning target. One student asked if she could try for high mastery of her Reconstruction learning target by helping a peer better connect the annotated bibliography document he had created to the current project. Another group of students chattered about the Bill of Rights, discussing the children's book they would be writing to prove the learning targets associated with the Constitution.

As a history "gatekeeper" for the school, Amy provided students a variety of ways to prove mastery of their learning targets, including making and defending a timeline, doing a "show and explain" interview, writing an iSearch essay, or even making and publishing a video. The most popular method, however, was what she called "rippling," where after one student proved mastery via a "show and explain," that student then taught a peer, and if the peer could in turn prove mastery, the first student could get high mastery.

As she circulated the room, asking probing questions, providing "crumbs," listening for misconceptions, and guiding students to scaffolding activities she thought would be ideal for their individual growth, she also updated her CBE progress report in real time via her iPad. This allowed the students to see their progress for each learning target immediately, in a color-coded fashion.

Even after being at SOWLA for three years, she still wanted to call it a grade book, even though there were no traditional grades on it. At one point she stepped back, took a breath, and observed that 100 percent of her students were engaged in conversations about history and the project. It was chaotic, it was messy, it was loud, but it was learning like she had come to expect at SOWLA. "Another day in paradise," she thought.

Students hardly realized it was time to head to their flex schedule class until she reminded them. Some students stayed—the ones she knew needed more one-on-one support—while most hurried off to their next block. The students coming in on this day were primarily ones taking her History I class and knew that it was the day for one of two Socratic Smackdowns (debates where a score is kept for each type of contribution) that took place each quarter. These were always popular and provided yet another way Amy could verify the depth of knowledge of her students.

As a tie-in with the project, the focus of the discussion was the ethics of sharecropping in the Reconstruction South and its implications for food security. She was really impressed with how students crafted elegant arguments that showed an impressive depth of knowledge. These same students, most of them "year 1" students at SOWLA, had been scared out of their wits just a few months ago when she did her first smackdown! Amy could now feel their passion as they debated each other over the quality of their evidence. The period was over before they knew it. PBL time!

Amy conferred with Ms. Greeley as she entered the room. They cotaught every PBL time to ensure that a humanities and STEM teacher were always present to answer any student questions. Luis's group was the main topic of discussion, though they also agreed to talking points for their individual rounds, where they spoke with the team leader of each PBL group.

They decided to let Luis, his team's leader, attempt to resolve the issue with one of the team members using the conflict resolution framework the teachers had trained students on earlier that year. They also agreed that one of them would step in if the conflict remained unresolved by the midpoint of the period. They then circulated around the room to provide feedback about the quality of websites, blogs, social media campaigns, and final prototypes, then watched mock pitches from a couple of groups to be sure they were all ready for the exhibition. They ended the period by giving each team a targeted pep talk to encourage nervous students.

Next, it was time for the staff meeting. Unlike the dreaded meetings at her old school, where she felt the teachers were only talked to, Amy always looked forward to her Critical Friends Group. All the learning guides got together to share best practices, debrief on instructional rounds, provide in-house professional development, and solve school-wide issues. Today, Amy shared results from her Socratic Smackdown and received feedback based on the National School Reform Faculty's "Focus Point" protocol from Mr. Jansen about a recent class he had observed. They had agreed in the preobservation conference that her point of emphasis would be getting more insight into the quality and rigor of student-to-student conversations.

Next came the planning session for the upcoming project, which a group of students had pitched to the group. Mr. Bridges, the principal, volunteered to coordinate the entry event, saying that the learning guides had more pressing issues. The group broke into smaller subteams, following their usual "divide and conquer" approach, before coming back together as a team to discuss what each subteam had developed. Today's subteams were focused on final product criteria, key quality-check milestones, and identifying potential mentors and local business collaborations. Finally, they called in the student event planning committee to discuss the final logistics for the exhibition night. The students walked them through the plan and answered any questions the group had. Everything was ready to go for the evening's program!

The SOWLA exhibition nights seemed to get more attention each time. The surrounding community was always curious to see what students would come up with, and the local media always knew they could find amazing stories to tell their respective audiences. This one was no exception! The food pantry had agreed to host it at their facility to showcase the robust partnership forged by the project. Students had set up their tables throughout the warehouse while everyone was encouraged to bring donations for the food bank.

Hundreds of people started entering the room before the event officially began. Students rushed to set up their tables, knowing that every visitor would receive a rubric and suggested questions that would test their academic knowledge, their public speaking ability, and the quality of their final product. Amy spent her time chatting with students to offer them encouragement and helpful hints, and to gauge their connection of their projects to her history class.

Amy also ran into various teachers from other schools, many from other districts and a couple from local universities, who praised the remarkable SOWLA students. They commented on how confident the students were and on their surprise at the quality of ideas and execution they observed. Amy gave them her card with her website on it reminded them that because the project was on the OER Commons, they were free to remix and use it to suit their own needs. They mentioned a few constraints that would make it impossible to implement anything like this at their schools—a sentiment Amy had heard often. Nevertheless, Amy offered to help these educators in any way she could, anytime they wanted to collaborate.

She circulated through the room and saw the incredible diversity of people SOWLA was bringing together in celebration of student work. She held back tears as she felt a familiar mix of pride, joy, and purpose that emerged from seeing what these young people were doing. Their passion to change the world was palpable, and they were doing it! This was the indescribable magic that enchanted every SOWLA staff member and imbued them with the energy they brought to their classrooms every day. What she saw this night was exactly why she had decided to become a teacher.

THE ADMINISTRATOR'S JOURNEY

Like most principals, David Bridges started as a teacher, first at a traditional elementary school and then at a magnet middle school with a STEM focus. Early in his tenure at the STEM school, the staff decided to become an officially designated Teacher-Powered School. This had given David a unique perspective on school leadership. The school had sought this designation because of its purported effects on student engagement and teacher collaboration. David had witnessed these effects firsthand and vowed that if he ever became a school administrator, he would embody the role of a teacher-powered leader.

Namely, he would view his role as a facilitator, culture cultivator, and catalyst who elicited feedback and ideas from his team rather than issuing top-down directives and enforcing compliance with his staff. So, when he had opportunity five years earlier to become SOWLA's principal, David jumped at the chance! He saw how Open Way Learning was clearly built on a teacher-powered, student-centered framework and was excited to be in on the ground floor.

He has worked hard ever since to take the culture to the next level: working with his teachers to be more inclusive of student voices, replacing restrictive rules with mutual accountability, and eliminating heavy-handed disciplinary actions and replacing them with a restorative justice model. These were big changes, even for a forward-thinking school like SOWLA! Years after its founding, SOWLA was still finding its footing in this suburban district dominated by other much larger and more traditional schools.

Today was a big day for his school. He was keenly aware that SOWLA was under intense pressure to continue producing strong results in order to remain a viable and supported choice for families in the community. Fortunately, despite the staff's absolute refusal to do anything remotely close to traditional "teaching to the test," SOWLA's test scores were consistently at the top of the district's accountability metrics. So, while he prided himself on SOWLA's 100 percent graduation rate and its college staying rate that was double the national average, the exhibition nights were, in his opinion, the true measure of this school's quality.

It was during these events that these students, each here through a zip code–based lottery that ensured the school's demographics reflected the community it served, were able to shine and prove to all the skeptics that this form of teaching and learning was undoubtedly preparing them to collaborate and compete with anyone on the planet. David had spent the last two years aggressively building SOWLA's network of local, national, and international collaborators. Consequently, exhibition nights had become increasingly popular. Tonight would be no exception.

David's morning started by responding to press inquiries about the school. His blog, website, and Twitter feed had become highly influential, so there was a steady stream of journalists, policy makers, and educators eager to speak to him about SOWLA. He finalized the details of an upcoming interview and then sent out a reminder call and email to parents and other potential attendees for the exhibition night. Afterward, he turned his attention to requesting another district waiver one of the student teams had brought to his attention and that the Critical Friends Group agreed needed to be changed. He found he had to do quite a few of these, but he leveraged the strong reputation the school had built to request such waivers from the local school board.

When the SOWLA teachers had come up with the idea for flexible schedules and skills labs based on student needs, the district—and some parents—had questioned the idea's merit. This had never been done before: What would the implications be if it didn't work? They had even asked David whether he should try to "rein in" his teachers and get back to basics. Instead of capitulating, David met with the superintendent to get buy-in, then presented the proposal to the school board along with the metrics they would track and the contingency plans they would follow.

He also coordinated a series of informational meetings with parents and teachers to be sure all parties completely understood the plan, and he developed follow-up actions to keep all stakeholders completely informed of what to expect and how results would be measured and communicated. Thankfully, he had persuaded all involved! That just confirmed what one of his old mentors had told him: strong results produce strong credibility.

Time and again, David found that he needed to be a shield for his school. The innovative practices that characterized SOWLA were often so unorthodox that they had been called into question. David was consistently tactful and insistent that the practices were effective, even if unfamiliar to him. He developed a deep sense of trust in his teachers and knew that their daily, direct interaction with the school's "customers," its students, made them ideally suited to execute solutions to any student learning or behavioral issue that would come up. He also respected the teachers enough to know that if they made a decision or a proposal, they would have considered all possibilities; even if it failed, he knew they would work to iterate on the idea and make it better for the students.

The district could not deny that the school's strong, consistent results and student work, as exemplified by exhibitions, were impressive. Moreover, the school was beginning to garner state and national recognition as a model of excellence, not only because of its results but also because of the relentless desire the school's staff had for sharing practices they knew worked with other educators through their digital and in-person networks. Nevertheless, at the end of the day, SOWLA was still expected to comply with whatever accountability requirements and top-down initiatives the federal government, state, or district was currently pushing. Although it was at times exhausting, he proudly embraced his role as filter and shield from bureaucratic minutiae so his teachers and students could focus on creating magic.

David was interrupted by a student discipline issue, a rare occurrence at SOWLA because of exceptional student engagement. This student had refused to do his English work because he was on the precipice of dropping out and his home life was falling apart. David had already visited this student's home and was acutely aware of his struggles. Instead of giving him detention or berating him for his irresponsibility, David set up a meeting with a machinist from a local engineering company that was on SOWLA's business advisory council, then arranged a Skype call with an Australian engineer he had met at an Open Way Learning conference.

This student was passionate about rebuilding cars but had failed the automotive classes SOWLA had arranged for him at the local community college. David thought meeting with a machinist and envisioning another possible career path might motivate him. The guidance counselor would take the student to meet the machinist at the factory later that day. David also made it clear that the student needed to meet with the English teacher and counselor later to restore trust and credibility in these relationships.

After a couple of hours at his desk, in an unpretentious space he had strategically set up near the commons area so that he could constantly see the bustle of student and staff activity, David started his daily rounds in the school's work spaces. As a former teacher, this was always his favorite part of the day and sometimes became most of his day. Teacher-powered "cadres" eased the load of administrative duties that plagued most other principals and allowed him to focus on building stronger relationships and networks of support with staff and students. Today, David was delighted to see the culmination of the quarter-long project and could tell that this work had sparked a lot of passion in the students.

From there it was off to the Critical Friends meeting, where David had an equal seat at the table with his teachers. When some of his fellow principals asked him if he was offended by such an arrangement, he would always reply

"Of course not!" and then would refer them to the school's long book study list on distributed leadership, innovation, and organizational excellence.

He used the Critical Friends venue to get a pulse on how things were going and to empower his teachers to collaborate and share ideas that could help the school better meet its mission. He knew that finding ways to enable more trust and transparency was critical to the team's ability to innovate and better respond to the needs of each student. He would routinely add his own ideas and suggestions, but always in a way that was consistent with his strong belief in the organization's approach to consensus and meritocracy.

Only rarely in his five years as principal had he needed to intervene and make a decision to breech an impasse, and even then he made sure it was done in a completely open manner, justifying the process to all parties so that trust was maintained. After helping to cultivate the school's Open Way Learning culture to the point where it was in the bones of every one of the school's stakeholders, he knew it would survive any organizational changes, including his departure—although he had no desire to go anywhere!

At this meeting, he volunteered to arrange the entry event for the next project, which would be a panel of experts on climate change. David knew he could leverage his network to convene this panel and didn't want his teachers to get bogged down with event planning.

Upon returning to his work space, David tweeted a teaser about the next project and posted a student-made flyer about exhibition night on the school's Facebook page. He had some excellent photos of student work, taken during his rounds, that he used to promote the event. He rounded out his afternoon by planning the agenda for the business advisory council meeting the following week, then continued work on a grant to add a laser-cutting machine to SOWLA's makerspace—a request that a student made the previous quarter.

As he walked to exhibition night, David felt the inevitable butterflies in his stomach that always preceded these events. The butterflies reminded him that trusting students and teachers to make the school successful required daily practice in patience, humility, and optimism. Before he knew it, the event had begun, and he found himself surrounded by excited parents, colleagues, and community partners. He took the opportunity to recruit new business advisory council members, to grant interviews to the reporters attending the event, and to see every student project and offer constructive feedback.

While starting his car to go home, David felt goose bumps as he reflected on the evening. He was overwhelmed with gratitude to be a part of a team that was changing lives every day. SOWLA not only prepared students to become the change makers and innovators today's world demands but also imbued its entire network of supporters with a renewed hope for the future. David was in awe once again of the enormous capacity displayed by SOWLA's staff and students. He cherished being able to tell their story and support their efforts.

THE PARENT'S JOURNEY

Roderigo was no stranger to adversity. The father of four had worked incredibly hard to build the life he envisioned for his family. Indeed, he had almost died on his two-week trek through the Arizona desert seventeen years ago to try to support his family back in Peru. After spending his family's life savings to pay a smuggler $15,000 to get him into the United States, the pressure was on. As he trudged through the desert, the memory of his tearful mother and siblings waving goodbye to him from their dirt-floored shack outside Lima played repeatedly in his head.

After arriving, Roderigo had worked six or seven days a week doing any job that was available, working at agriculture, factory work, meat processing plants, painting, and construction. He met his wife a year after arriving, and they started a family. In addition to providing the necessities for his own wife and family, Roderigo sent money to Peru each month for his mother and siblings, who had begun to depend on the extra income.

His oldest son, Luis, was his pride and joy. Generally, Luis was a very reserved and shy young man, but he had a powerful intellect and an enduring compassion for others. Though Roderigo had only finished his fifth grade education before starting full-time work on the family's coffee farm, Luis was destined for a different path. Roderigo relentlessly encouraged and supported Luis to pursue the finest education available in the area.

Roderigo's work experiences had given him a solid idea about what a fine education would look like. He had consistently worked the lowest-wage jobs in the area and had lost a couple due to automation, so he knew that his value as a strong-backed, rule-following, hard worker didn't command the same wages as his more well-educated coworkers. However, he also knew about the importance of communicating and solving problems in any line of work, so he wanted to ensure that Luis's education reflected that reality. So, when Roderigo heard about a school that was teaching students how to collaborate, be creative, think critically, and build wide networks outside the school walls, he knew he wanted his children to go there.

Once Luis began attending SOWLA, Roderigo saw a new child gradually emerge. Though all of the school's policies and approaches were confusing at first because they were so different, Roderigo began to trust the process because of its impact on his child and the frequent contact from the school's staff. Luis's most recent project had him particularly energized, and Roderigo couldn't wait to attend the exhibition night.

When the night finally arrived, Roderigo had to leave the factory early, which he knew would cut into his hourly earnings. He knew it would be worth it as soon as he walked into the food bank where the event was being held. Every table seemed to be a gold mine of information and knowledge. Roderigo was particularly impressed with how one group had connected their project to their Spanish curriculum by creating questions to ask a class in Guatemala and learning about how food worked in their community. After wading through the crowd, Roderigo spotted Luis surrounded by more than twenty strangers.

He walked up to see his son—his shy, reserved son—dazzling the audience with his insight and knowledge. Roderigo listened intently, though some of Luis's words were hard to comprehend because of the advanced knowledge they conveyed. Still, Roderigo was overcome with emotion after witnessing his child. It was at that point that Roderigo was confident that Luis would never have to endure the circumstances that his father had fought against his entire life and that he had a skill set that would lead to his success.

GETTING REAL

> I believe that two things are true. It is true, as would-be reformers often argue, that statutes, policies, rules, regulations, contracts, and case law make it tougher than it should be for school and system leaders to drive improvement and, well, lead. However, it is also the case that leaders have far more freedom to transform, reimagine, and invigorate teaching, learning, and schooling than is widely believed.—Rick Hess, author of *The Cage-Busting Teacher*

Do the vignettes of Luis, Amy, and David sound too good to be true? Engaged students, wide networks of supporters, sharing a school story far and wide, distributed leadership, teacher collaboration, student-centered learning, trusting administrators, buy-in to a shared vision at all levels—this is all the stuff of educational theorists, right? Well, the entire picture we painted above is in action at many schools around the world. One such school, Tri-County Early College, is the template for this narrative and embodies much of the Open Way Learning Academy (OWLA) framework. Though it's not always so picture perfect and positive, it is happening, and it is powerful stuff!

The OWLA framework is not simply the school model at TCEC and other innovative schools across the world; rather, it encompasses commonly cited characteristics of the most successful schools in the educational landscape, which practice deep collaboration, rapid innovation and scaling, and sharing at every level—on the web and in person. What are the common threads for successful schools? All are directly or indirectly what we define as Open Way Learning organizations by demonstrating the following:

- A shared vision of excellence
- A commitment to true distributed leadership
- A deep culture of collaboration, sharing, and continuous improvement and innovation

Those characteristics create the foundation for a powerful teaching and learning environment, especially when coupled with these:

- A coherent instructional framework that relies on high standards, high expectations, and strong support mechanisms[1]
- A highly capable faculty and staff that are fully committed to individual and collective improvement
- A school culture that is passionately student-centered
- Strong ties between the school and partners outside of the school—local and global—enhanced with solid technology

Do these criteria sound familiar? If not, read the narratives at the beginning of this chapter again and see if you can find every one of these characteristics in action. Once you see how they are manifested in this admittedly hypothetical scenario, you will better understand the next section—about how they are also characteristics of the OWLA framework.

CHARACTERISTICS OF EXCELLENT SCHOOLS

Intelligence looks for what is known to solve problems. Creativity looks for what is unknown to discover possibilities.—Simon Senik

Educational experts know what works—not only in individual classrooms, but in schools, districts, and networks. For example, in 1998 McREL issued a report authored by Robert Marzano entitled, "A Theory-Based Meta-Analysis of Research on Instruction," that analyzed, compared, and summarized over one hundred different studies that involved over four thousand comparisons of experimental and control groups.[2]

Moreover, John Hattie, professor of education and director of the Melbourne Education Research Institute at the University of Melbourne, Australia, conducted an extensive meta-analysis on performance indicators within education and developed a way of ranking their relative effect on various student outcomes. His book, *Visible Learning*, is the result of a groundbreaking study where he analyzed and compiled findings from hundreds of meta-analyses of thousands of studies of over eighty million students to develop a measure of effect on over 130 influences on learning.[3]

It's worth noting that researchers such as Marzano and Hattie have not found a single, one-size-fits-all model that is right for all students and all contexts—the proverbial silver bullet. These analyses, however, do substantiate a growing and compelling body of evidence that illuminates the characteristics of successful schools. Moreover, there are a number of school networks, philanthropic organizations, education think tanks, and researchers that have invested significant time and resources to identify factors that have the most positive impact on students.

Not surprisingly, given that the OWL approach has evolved using data analysis and iteration on existing best practices, there is also a common thread that runs between these characteristics of success and the OWL framework. This alignment was verified with an analysis of the published data from fourteen such sources looking at the specific attributes highlighted in this book. We summarize this analysis to show you how the Open Way Learning Academy model can synthesize, strengthen, and clarify a critical few of these success factors so that they can be implemented with fidelity and at scale.

Table 6.1 was compiled using the findings of various well-reputed organizations that work intensively in the education arena and using research by subject matter experts in education (details for each are available on the openwaylearning.org website). This is not intended to be an exhaustive list of all such sources, and the characteristics listed are not the only ones these sources endorse.

If you are a stakeholder who can influence a school or district to successfully establish the fundamental OWL characteristics described here, you will have cleared the path for an easier, more rapid, and more sustainable implementation of one or more of these best practice models. In doing so, the goal of writing this book will have been met: you will have the inspiration and methodology to help a school start and maintain its journey to educational excellence by leveraging an open-source ethos through the Open Way. Ideally, your story will then illuminate what can be done and influence others to do the same, ultimately quickening the pace to create the positive subversion of this massive and complex machine we call public education. Even if you are the only one to use this information and you influence only one school or even one classroom, the effort will have been worthwhile.

Table 6.1. Characteristics of Great Schools

Characteristics of excellent schools	Open Way Learning strategy
Coherent instructional system with rigorous and relevant expectations	Collaborative teachers design and implement a consistent instructional framework that may include school-wide practices such as project-based learning and competency-based education. These practices challenge students and increase relevance across the curriculum.
Student-centered, personalized learning with a climate of care	Giving students voice and choice in projects and when demonstrating content mastery while including them in school decision-making processes creates a student-centered atmosphere. Then, providing advisory supports along with flexible scheduling shows a school's commitment to responding to their needs.
High-performing, collaborative faculty focused on continuous development and improvement	Making a school teacher-powered ensures that important decisions are made by on-the-ground personnel, while regular, high-quality PLC meetings provide a venue for professional development and reflection. Also, empowering teachers to respond to student needs quickly by creating innovative solutions drives continuous improvement.
Ties between family, community, and school	By requiring mentors on every project and using pedagogy that emphasizes real-world relevance and service learning, students naturally connect their schoolwork to the outside world and widen the school's network of supporters.
Culture of inquiry, innovation, collaboration, and exploration	Focusing collaborative student work on authentic problems and questions encourages exploration and inquiry. The OWL model emphasizes innovation and failing forward in every task.
Systems for collecting and exchanging knowledge effectively	Using blogs, websites, and social media to promote and deepen learning, while also providing authentic assessments on those tasks, ensures that student work has a public profile available to other students, educators, and community members.
Strong leadership and shared ownership	Teacher-powered governance structures build leadership capacity in teachers and cultivate a deep sense of ownership across the entire staff. For shared ownership to work, OWL requires a shared vision that is frequently renegotiated and refined by all stakeholders.

This table connects school design principles endorsed by various leading educational organizations and philanthropists with practices used in Open Way Learning.

NEVER OUT OF REACH

We hope that after reading this chapter, which offers a blueprint of the Open Way Learning Academy model, you are feeling inspired to start the OWL fire in your own sphere of influence. No action is too small to create a spark. Recognize that your context may demand a variation of the portrait presented here. That is expected!

Just as Linux has been the source code for a diverse array of software applications, the OWLA template can be considered your local school's kernel, which can then be adapted and customized in a way that meets your community's specific needs. Indeed, if collaboration, free exchange, and innovation are at its heart, Open Way Learning can take many forms.

7

Be the Spark

Never doubt that a small group of thoughtful, committed citizens can change the world; indeed, it's the only thing that ever has.—Margaret Mead

Don't we see the need for change? Don't we see the explicit link between the quality of our schools and the future economic prosperity of our own communities and country? Are there not enough education stakeholders willing to demand structural changes from our policy makers?

Perhaps. Then again, perhaps not. There is a strong possibility that we are more comfortable with what we've always done than we realize. After all, it takes more energy to confront the school board or central office than it does to remain quiet. It takes more work to give up planning time and ask the teacher across the hall to collaborate on a cotaught lesson than it does to just do our own thing in our own room. It takes significantly more time and effort to plan a new and engaging project-based unit than to simply rely on the canned lesson or textbook with all its worksheets and teacher guides.

Frankly, it's much easier, and unfortunately acceptable, to blame the student struggling to keep up with the curriculum than to build a relationship with him. Why should we try to find a way to make a connection when others have not? After all, we did our job by covering the material. If he didn't pay attention, tough. Maybe he'll grow up next year.

Did any of that make you uncomfortable? Most of us would rather not be the person who steps between a woman wearing a hijab and the bigot screaming at her. We might think we would do the right thing, but, then again, isn't it easier to look the other way, pretend it's not happening, and get off the train at the next stop? The cost of comfort is the perpetuation of the status quo, and in this profession the stakes are simply too high to allow that to continue.

Robyn Hoyton, a nationally recognized teacher from the Brandywine School District in Delaware, offers this perspective:

> When I look around my community to help students find possible careers, I see clear evidence of a need for change. Technology has implications for everyone from a car mechanic to a CEO. The ability of anyone to go online and learn about any topic has changed the necessary skills for being successful. Because education involves people, we can't just create one-size-fits-all solutions that will work for every student. An open-source framework allows educators to share successful learning activities and lessons with our peers. This then helps us all be more effective in meeting the needs of individual students.

It's said that when one door closes, another one opens. The impetus behind this book—its naive optimism, one might say—is our belief that when enough people are willing to leave behind the comfortable model where collaboration, open sharing, and innovation are an exception rather than the rule, then we find a path that leads to an exciting new normal. Acquiescing to the past is always easier. It's why we see essentially the same structural foundation in our schools that existed one hundred years ago and why the frenetic pace of innovation driven by open-source technologies has not made the same level of change happen in our education systems.

To put it plainly, you are being asked to be a subversive, like Martin Luther King, Lincoln, Mandela, Bolívar, Newton, and Darwin, as well as some lesser-known disruptors such as the educators who contributed their examples to this book. You are being asked to disrupt the status quo and begin the journey to establish an Open Way Learning culture within your own school, district, and beyond. Light the spark, build the tinder, and create a campfire—and, with some help and luck, you can turn it into a bonfire.

RESISTING CHANGE

In their book *Immunity to Change*, Robert Kagen and Lisa Laskow Lahey cite a recent study in which physicians tell heart patients that if they don't change their habits, they will die.[1] Even knowing this information, only one in seven successfully make the change. Changing the status quo is difficult, even when the stakes are life or death.

Passionate educators all over the world are doing everything they know to better serve the individual needs of their students. They are having hard conversations focused on doing whatever it takes to make a difference, including using many of the best practices mentioned in this book. Nevertheless, even with all this hard work, change remains elusive. Why?

Chip Heath and Dan Heath's book *Switch* is a wonderful guide that may answer this question and an excellent reference for any education stakeholder looking to effect change. They use the metaphor of a person riding an elephant down a path and describe how to create change by directing the "rider," or the *minds* of stakeholders, by painting a clear vision and eliminating confusion; by directing the "path," or managing the *environment* to promote success; and then by convincing the "elephant," or the *emotional side* of changemakers, through the use of emotional experiences to foster buy-in. If any of these three elements isn't considered, the Heaths claim, change efforts are doomed to fail.[2]

The "path" for educators can be challenging. Time, energy, and passion can be eroded by the flood of rules, procedures, habits, regulations, and attitudes woven into the current system. Is it any wonder that rather than championing change, educators slowly retreat behind closed doors, into what Frederick Hess calls "the cage," waiting for someone else to be the champion?[3]

Hess, a resident scholar and the director of education policy studies at the American Enterprise Institute, reminds us in his provocative and inspirational book, *The Cage-Busting Teacher*, that a true leader finds a way to break out of this cage—a cage often made worse by our own assumptions and inaction. Such a leader looks for the fissures in the system to ensure great teaching

CULTURE EATS STRATEGY FOR BREAKFAST.
—PETER DRUCKER

It's an important point to be reminded why there was such an emphasis on mission and vision earlier in the book. As the quote above so succinctly states, if a culture for change is not present, one will face significant headwinds when starting the OWL fire. This is not to dissuade you, but it is a pragmatic reality. The good news, is that you can be the agent for change by focusing on small wins that distinguish you from the past, by building your capabilities and those of your peers, and by highlighting to others that a change is underway (branding 101). With a tenacious focus on a long term vision of excellence, success will breed success, strengths will outweigh setbacks, and the culture reaches a tipping point. We live in a world where change is all around us, so people already know how to adapt to change. The trick is to proactively create an environment where those same people see embracing change as part of your school's strategy for the future. That's when culture and strategy are aligned. To use another Drucker quote: "In a period of rapid structural change the only organizations that survive are the 'change leaders.'" You are that change leader.

is being supported, builds a solution-focused atmosphere for the team, and stretches the limits of funding and authority to ensure maximum benefit for students. In other words, she takes full advantage of the freedom from the cage to challenge the status quo.

STARTING THE FIRE

You may feel overwhelmed with the implications of this task, but take heart! Think about the various stages of OWL implementation such as building a fire (see figure 7.1). You start small to create a sustainable base before adding the big logs. Think of this part of the book as a guide to build the Open Way Learning fire from any position in a formal or informal educational setting.

Perhaps you are in one of the hostile environments that too many educators inhabit nowadays. Are you in a school with an overbearing principal who squashes teacher initiatives or in a school where teachers keep to themselves, calling you an "overachiever" whenever you offer a new idea? Are you a principal in a district that micromanages schools based on test scores or a parent frustrated by the lack of a forward-thinking vision for your community's schools? Bottom line: if you think other stakeholders will not be as excited for OWL as you are, you will have to provide the spark and the tinder that engage their interest.

The OWL model is immune to meddling from the self-perpetuating hierarchy if squarely pointed at peer relationships. Teachers could ask other teachers for advice or offer to coteach an interdisciplinary lesson or unit. Administrators could bring SRI protocols to a staff meeting and offer to facilitate. You will need to choose your collaborators wisely—open-minded, student-centered educators with a disposition toward change. Invest your energy in them first.

The key is to work with what you have. If teacher isolation is an issue at your school, then use it to your advantage by trying out innovative OWL teaching methods in your own classroom, even if traditionalist colleagues scoff. Shift the onus of responsibility and decision-making to the students through project-based learning, competency-based education, and individualized, student-centered approaches.

Establish a norm that student work is never just busywork or only for the teacher. Provide targeted feedback on activities that truly scaffold a student's depth of knowledge to a standard in lieu of traditional grading. Assess this depth of knowledge with authentic performance assessments, ideally with a public audience. Create assessments that gauge how well students share their work online. Encourage students to recruit mentors outside the school and then create assignments that require them to get feedback from their mentors.

Lighting the
Open Way Learning Fire

Spark	Campfire	Bonfire
-Work towards creating effective PLC's using SRI protocols -Try out more innovative teaching methods, then share what you're learning -Share and learn from social media networks -Blog about your successes and struggles so others can learn from you -Share your lessons and resources freely with others	-Create a standing agenda and teacher committees to push forward new projects and initiatives -Tap the collective teacher wisdom to design in-house professional development -Create a Business Advisory Council -Start creating school-wide / interdisciplinary projects -Have a book club with this book to get on the same page about OWL	-Network with other OWL schools or other innovative networks like Opportunity Culture, EdVestors, or Teacher-Powered Schools -Conduct school visits to other schools using interesting models -Encourage district leaders to adopt systemic initiatives like district-wide PLCs -Collaborate on projects with other schools, organizations, and businesses -Present at conferences and maintain excellent social media / web presence

Figure 7.1.   This shows how Open Way Learning can be implemented in any environment with small steps or huge leaps.

Sharing your work with others in person or online will pay dividends. Create a Twitter account and start following innovative educators. When something exciting happens in your school, tell your network a story with photos or video (refer to the openwaylearning.org website for a photo release template). For your most compelling insights, write a blog post. You can host this on your own website or offer a guest post for a variety of organizations eager for excellent, innovative content. Edutopia, the Center for Teaching Quality, EdWeek, ASCD, and TeachingPartners' National Blogging Collaborative are all venues for teachers to share their ideas.

You should also consider formatting projects and assignments in ways that can be used by other teachers, then share them freely. Post these assignments on a public website or on OER Commons so that others can adapt them for their own contexts. This also increases the potential for collaboration with colleagues, at your local school and elsewhere, who will appreciate you giving them compelling ideas to use in their own classrooms.

These are all relatively easy ways to a more open school—examples teachers can use in their own classrooms, administrators can support directly or behind the scenes, and parents can support through advocacy. Once the OWL shift has been made, students will start talking about the exciting things happening in their classes and others will be curious. You will become the brave soul who starts the fire on a chilly morning while everyone else lingers in their cozy sleeping bags, afraid to start the day. Eventually, you will be able to throw some kindling on the fire. Before long, others will unzip their tents and join you around the fire ring. If you build it, they will come!

KINDLING THE FLAMES

Open Way Learning may find traction in environments where a handful of staff members are already using its methods, or are at least inclined to welcome change. For these situations, OWL practitioners may be able to help their organizations reach a "tipping point," where an entire staff might buy into an OWL Academy framework.

Much of the central work of OWL implementation at the department or school level can happen in a professional learning community (PLC). You can ensure that these meetings realize their full potential and highest efficiency by adding positive structure with trained facilitation, norms, and protocols, including a prohibition on nonconstructive criticism. Create a standing agenda that ensures that sharing, giving feedback, and engaging in professional development are all part of the framework. With these enablers in place, you will naturally have deeper conversations about student learning.

This may also be the time to begin building a support network for a reno-vated school model—perhaps starting in your department or even an "OWL Academy" within a school. Contact local businesses to see if they would support the school through mentorship and internships for students. Hold meetings with them to share the exciting things students are doing, ask them for input on how to deepen student learning, and inquire about other kinds of support they might offer.

Teachers could play with the idea of creating department or school-wide interdisciplinary projects. This structure can expedite the adoption of better teaching methods and build institutional capacity by pairing OWL practitio-ners with nonpractitioners. The relationships built in the process of cocreation are crucial to effective collaboration, which is foundational to Open Way Learning. Each project could then be posted on the school website to empha-size the sharing culture.

Share the narratives from chapter 6 with colleagues, perhaps via a book study, to spark the discussion (see the openwaylearning.org website for ques-tion prompts). This can start dialogue that leads to a revised shared vision

TEACHER LEADERSHIP

This book has highlighted a number of examples of how teachers can drive change. There are many others, but they all have one common element: teachers have to step up, take a risk, be vulnerable, and be a leader. Lead from the classroom without leaving the classroom.

And no, being a teacher leader is not an extra duty like bus monitoring; a teacher leader is a natural leader, as mentioned in chapter 1, that the orga-nization organically looks to for guidance and inspiration. Such a leader not only self-identifies as a leader, regardless of role, but leads people through influence, demands respect through professionalism, relentlessly shares knowledge with colleagues in and out of school, is constantly on the lookout for teaching improvements, is keenly aware of the latest educational trends (technology, best practices, policy, and so on), and, above all, is willing to engage with the community, school management, and policy makers to fight for changes that help the school continue to meet its vision of excellence.

Fortunately, the National Board for Professional Teaching Standards, the National Education Association, and the Center for Teaching Quality have collaborated to produce the comprehensive document *The Teacher Leader-ship Competencies* to ensure the term "teacher leader" doesn't devolve into another eduspeak buzzword.[1]

1. *The Teacher Leadership Competencies* (Center for Teaching Quality, National Board for Professional Teaching Standards, and the National Education Association, 2018), http://www.nbpts.org/wp-content/uploads/teacher_leadership_competencies_final.pdf.

for the school—one that includes input from all members of the learning community and more accurately meets the needs of its members. Facilitating conversations about the mission and vision of the school in the context of OWL could prove very fruitful in reaching a tipping point.

FUELING THE BONFIRE

If the preceding sections describe steps you have already taken, it is time to create a bonfire, send some smoke signals, and influence the entire educational ecosystem. Some schools may be a long way down the path toward becoming an OWL Academy (OWLA). OWL is intrinsically influential because of its emphasis on collaboration and the free exchange of innovative ideas. If the narratives in chapter 6 already sound familiar, now is the time to set high expectations for how every staff member and student participates in a wider network.

Expanding influence means expanding networks. Finding other OWL academies can be a primary strategy for enhancing the teaching and learning at your local school. If your school is already part of a formal national or regional network such as Opportunity Culture, New Tech Network, EdVestors, or the like, then this is much easier. You can reach out to other schools within such networks that likely share your disposition toward change.

If you are not part of such a network, you can begin to build an informal network by reaching out to other schools and educators through social media or via the openwaylearning.org website (refer to the Pockets of Excellence project described in chapter 3). If possible, visit other innovative schools that are practicing OWL methodologies so you can see it firsthand. The key is to see actual working examples with students so you have the opportunity to change your paradigm—something Thomas Kuhn defined over fifty years ago.[4]

Without making the effort to see what change looks like, chances are you will only be "innovating" around the edges, and that's not good enough. Creating and building organic network relationships will lead to intriguing new ideas and possibly even cotaught units with staff from other schools. Students at different schools could collaborate on the same project running in multiple OWLAs. This level of collaboration would create ample opportunity for mutually beneficial cross-pollination.

Staff at OWLAs should also start looking to impact larger networks such as their districts, states, or nations. Putting feelers out for other district schools interested in learning about OWL or collaborating with your school is a suitable place to start, and a primary purpose of the openwaylearning.org website. OWL Academy teachers could develop district-wide or network-wide PLCs, allowing OWL interest to grow organically as peers share ideas.

A CONVERSATION WITH ELLIOT WASHOR

One of the highlights in gathering stories for this book was speaking with some of the true pioneers and thought leaders in education, such as Elliot Washor, a cofounder of Big Picture Learning. Washor has been on the front lines of educational reform for over thirty-five years and continues to be in schools, working with students, staff, and communities almost every day.

He is also a popular writer and speaker who travels the world to help schools and school systems design and implement more engaging teaching and learning environments. The George Lucas Foundation recently selected Washor as one of "the Daring Dozen—the Twelve Most Daring Educators." The following are highlights from the conversation he had with Ben, specific to his experience with the themes discussed in this book:

- *Collaboration:* Washor reminded us to not underestimate the power of a network of people who have similar goals and passion. "One of the reasons Big Picture Learning has been so successful is its intense focus on sustainability and the leverage we could use based on the credibility we have built over time." He also pointed out that the term "network" could be too linear and that what is needed is a "meshwork" of people to people. "As Tim Ingold says, it's less about the "I" and more about the "we.""[1]
- *Shared Vision:* Big Picture Learning uses its ten distinguishers as a set of elements to pull their network together and distinguish it from most other schools.[2] But Washor also underscored the need to use such a framework within the context of each school's local community. "No single BPL school design is going to work everywhere. Each school has its own set of values that are consistent with its local conditions, so it is important to design them to fit the community."
- *Implementing Change:* Washor emphasized the need to clearly define and measure quality changes in schools. "It's really important for any change effort to consider how it will maintain quality. The methods you use to validate this quality must be rigorous, otherwise the core idea will become diluted over time. Preventing this will require constant attention and emphasis. The other thing to keep in mind is that most reformers are only focused on being marginally more successful as opposed to drastically more successful, which is obviously harder to do. Consider up front what your organization [is] ready for."
- *Sustaining Excellence:* "Any high-performing school must have a strong culture and a strong succession plan in order to ensure that the leadership continues to support and expand the school's mission."

1. Washor is drawing here on Tim Ingold, *Making: Anthropology, Archaeology, Art and Architecture* (New York: Routledge, 2014), 5–6.
2. "10 Distinguishers," Big Picture Learning, https://www.bigpicture.org/apps/pages /index.jsp?uREC_ID=389353&type=d&pREC_ID=902235.

Strongly consider encouraging or seeking certification for status as a Teacher-Powered School. This will engage the school with a wide support network that supports distributed leadership. Teachers can become Teacher-Powered ambassadors to further promote this approach—offering another venue for sharing and collaboration. Use this governance structure to deepen student and staff ownership of the direction of the school and to empower students and staff to be its champions.

Sharing must be second nature for an OWLA. Push the boundaries! Set the expectation that every student, teacher, and administrator be "published" in some way. Ask staff and students to write blog posts and press releases to promote their work or the OWL concept. Integrate sharing and collaboration into every project and help students connect with contacts outside the local community. Write op-eds or present at conferences about your experiences and results. And, of course, be willing to share resources with anyone who wants them. This is how crowdsourced Open Way Learning becomes a movement!

WRAPPING IT UP

The difference between a good educator and a great educator is that the former figures out how to work within the constraints of traditional policies and accepted assumptions, whereas the latter figures out how to change whatever gets in the way of doing right by kids.—Alfie Kohn

You see where this is going. You have the power to change in one small way. Today. In doing so, you help clear the path that honors the aspirations of each student. By making the choice to become an Open Way Learning practitioner, you are creating a spark that could start a powerful and transformative fire.

Be prepared for the potential fire extinguishers of self-doubt, stakeholder blowback, periodic failure, and resistance from those used to simply "doing school" the way it's always been done. When the firefighters come to put out your fire, recognize that you are not alone. There are so many supporters for you to lean on in your own community, school, district, or social network—and there's also a community of fellow readers who will be telling their stories on our website and through social media (#OpenWayLearning). Even if you feel like you're struggling to keep the embers lit, it won't be long before colleagues and students see the wisdom of your openness and start to join you. That's the trademark modus operandi of the open-source ethos—both within and outside of education.

By their very nature, innovative ideas are new and untested. This model is no exception. Ideally, this book will further "codify" Open Way Learning within the lexicon of education movements and lend it further credibility through future pedagogical research.

As you have seen, OWL is the combination of a multitude of research-based approaches with a built-in mechanism for scaling through open, crowdsourced, collective action that takes on a life of its own rather than thoughtlessly following a centralized leader, organization, or sanctioning body. That is in stark contrast to the myriad educational reform efforts that stop at the classroom walls. If we agree that the core purpose of education is to prepare children for the challenges of the future, then we need a tool appropriate for the future, not one rooted in the past.

> We learn from effective schools research that in good schools there is a shared commitment among staff to the school's mission and priorities. But we don't learn the process by which such a commitment can be created. It is sort of like buying a self-help book on running a restaurant and reading that serving good food is really important.—Grover J. "Russ" Whitehurst, who runs the education policy shop at the Brookings Institution and was director of the U.S. Department of Education's Institute of Education Sciences

This book illustrated how to create Open Way Learning environments any education stakeholder can use to initiate positive change in his or her own school context—ideally in a way that creates a model other schools would want to adopt. The fact that this is an open-source movement means it will not easily be bounded by traditional institutions and will likely take on a life of its own.

The goal has never been to create a one-size-fits-all solution that integrates nicely into every school and every district. Nor was it to somehow monetize this concept by creating a centralized "pay to play" network. The goal is to build a true, organic open-source community of like-minded stakeholders who know that it's time for a different approach.

There is simply no need to create a traditional, linear model when dealing with the elements of the Open Way. The OWL framework that is rooted in the characteristics described in this book will, by its nature, elicit the best ideas that are perfectly suited for the local context and individual needs of each learner. If you think about the concept of the "code talks" from chapter 1, you will recognize that details will emerge from the wisdom of the crowd—each community's practitioners and stakeholders—and not from the authors of this book (or any other outside entity, for that matter). This is the inherent power of the Open Way. The best ideas will float to the top, and as long as collaboration, free exchange of ideas, and a culture of innovation exist, they will always have the student squarely at the center.

Just as Linus Torvalds's original post about his free operating system eventually grew into the powerful open-source operating system Linux, one that can stand toe to toe with the likes of Microsoft and Apple, the work of this book is just the tip of the iceberg. It is part of a much larger movement to ensure every student on the planet has access to high-quality educational resources, unencumbered by legacy systems that knowingly or unknowingly put up barriers to this access (cost, location, obsolete materials, legal constraints, and so on).

Networks such as OpenSource.com, the Open Education Consortium, and the many others referenced throughout this book are already impacting schools and communities all over the world, bringing an ethos of open source to bear on these traditional institutions. This ambitious work is nothing short of democratizing education for all. Like democracy movements before it, this one has the unstoppable power of the people behind it. People like you, who are no longer willing to accept that the quality of children's education depends on geography, race, income, religion, disability, or any other characteristic other than the inherent drive and desire to learn.

If you are eager to become an Open Way Learning activist or practitioner, join our online network at openwaylearning.org and contribute your ideas for projects, approaches, and activities. The website also has many projects and documents we have created to help you implement Open Way Learning practices. You can follow us, Ben and Adam, on Twitter (@OpenWayLearning, @engineerteacher, and @adamhaigler). Share your own reactions and experiences using the hashtag #OpenWayLearning. If the virtual connection isn't sufficient, invite us to your conference, school, or organization to discuss how you could begin implementing this methodology. We are willing to do whatever it takes to help you become open-source agents for change!

The Open Education Consortium beautifully articulates the goal of opening up education with the following statement: "Sharing is probably the most basic characteristic of education: education is sharing knowledge, insights and information with others, upon which new knowledge, skills, ideas, and understanding can be built." Indeed. Your story and your voice are part of the work to make Open Way Learning a reality for every student. Let's get started.

Afterword

If you've reached this far in the book, it's a safe bet that you've been convinced by its arguments. Let's face it, if you haven't bought into its message by now, you'd have to be a masochist to have gotten this far. So, since you're not that reader, it's probably safe to assume that you're so fired up with practical ways to open up learning that you don't really have time for an afterword. I expect that you'll be eager to try out some of the books' many ideas with the young learners you work with, look after, or occasionally borrow.

So, I won't keep you.

On the off chance that you still have some lingering doubts, however, it falls to me to reassure you that should you decide to implement some aspect of open learning, you would not be alone.

Indeed, you'd be part of a global movement—one that reaches far beyond education. From corporations that have ripped up hierarchical org charts and replaced them with self-managing teams to people-powered public sector organizations, it sometimes feels like the whole world is going open. That's on my good days. On my bad days, I remind myself that Apple (a classic closed organization) is still one of the most profitable companies in the world and that when the so-called fake news that now dominates the news cycle is fact-checked and found wanting, it merely shrugs its shoulders.

From 2011 to 2013 I researched and wrote a book, *Open: How We'll Work, Live and Learn in the Future*. At the time, the concept of "openness"—in the context of learning, organizational structures, technology, and especially our mindsets—was not particularly present in public dialogue. In trying to defend a hypothesis—best summed up by the *Guardian* as "the free and open exchange of information has the power to change the world for the better"—I made a lot of forecasts. Paying no heed to the axiom that there are only two kinds of forecasters (lucky or wrong) I speculated that, in due course, politicians would be unable to keep secrets, that social media would enable individuals and clusters of enthusiasts to outsmart large corporations, and that learning would become more social, less tied to the classroom. My research period coincided with the fallout from the global financial crash, and at the time the Arab Spring was still full of righteous indignation and optimism. Few saw that, at least in the case of Syria, it would turn into a long, desolate winter.

One of the caveats I inserted into the book was that the technological revolution we're all experiencing is morally neutral. It simply holds up a mirror and says "this is who you are." It can be used for good or ill. Perhaps it was naive to assume that social media would become a transformative tool of bottom-up defiance. I believe it still is, but the intervening period has also seen it become an equally powerful tool for top-down political persuasion. Perhaps it was inevitable that Twitter and Facebook would be corrupted by groups like Cambridge Analytica and by presidents using it to spread chaos and confusion. In my defense, I also argued that the battle for "open" would always be in play, a continual struggle for transparency, not secrecy, and for collaboration to triumph over confrontation.

And that struggle will continue. However, the rationale behind my book was that, so far, the impact of the technological transformation has been more about values than valves, so the democratizing force behind this shift will withstand the periodic attempts to subvert it. To paraphrase Theodore Parker, the arc of the moral universe may be long, but it bends toward openness.

I guess it ultimately depends on how willing citizens, business leaders, politicians, and school leaders are to turn the unstoppable flow of information that we now experience into actions that make the world a better place. David Preston, in the foreword to this book, noted the tragedy of the Parkland, Florida, massacre. Personally, I watch the ethical passion fueling the survivors' attempts to bring about gun control and I'm filled with hope for the future. Open learning is as much about equity and social justice as it is about ensuring that knowledge flows and is shared. Otherwise, what's the point?

I described going open as an irreversible force because once people have enjoyed the greater control over their lives that sharing knowledge makes possible, they're not likely to give that up. And so it is with their learning.

To be philosophical for a moment, we learn, in large part, so that we can imagine how things can be made better. Those "things" may be a household life hack or a TED Talk on spirituality. The phenomenal growth of informal and social learning means that the sense of fulfillment experienced in helping others, or in feeling appreciated for your way with thoughts and words, is no longer the preserve of the wealthy elite, the intelligentsia, or the clerics. And those who used to wield influence and power are increasingly being held to account by the power of us. There's no route back to an age of deference.

Take the peace process in Northern Ireland as an example. It's been over twenty years since the Good Friday agreement was signed, bringing peace to a centuries-old hostility. It's been a bumpy road since then, but, however fractious the politics have been since 1998, it is considered socially unacceptable to even contemplate, let alone voice, going back to the polarization that flourished during "the troubles."

Historically, that polarization was stoked by priests, politicians, and paramilitaries. The ordinary people of Ulster—especially the millennials—have now found their voices. One could argue that, by doing so, they have demonstrated that a raft of expensive "peace dividend" education projects have been less impactful in promoting tolerance of the "other" than young people informally interacting, virtually and in person. As Finn Purdy, a teenage blogger from Belfast, put it: "The power of Snapchat or a Belfast nightclub against the backdrop of already changed attitudes have done far more to bring people together than the artificial setting of a cross community workshop."

My point is this: the open sharing of knowledge is a learning revolution that has precipitated a social and cultural revolution in which every voice counts. When you're on the receiving end of abuse from a gaggle of Twitter trolls (as I frequently am; educators can be surprisingly vindictive), it's easy to regret every voice counting. But for every attempted Twitter shaming, there are a dozen women adding to the collective power of #MeToo; for every businessman exposed as a fraudster, there are a million donations to justgiving.com. Let's also remember that the etiquette needed for social media to continue the job of reshaping cultural norms is still being collectively formed. But it's OK; we'll figure it out.

Why is any of this concluding a book about learning? In my view, schools aren't immune to this social and cultural revolution (no matter how much some folks might wish otherwise). Open learning may present many challenges, but it also provides a wealth of opportunity.

I visit schools all over the world and I feel for the many teachers I meet who recognize the immediacy of knowledge contained on every student's mobile device but are frustrated by the distractive effect of social media. They appreciate the authenticity that comes with great community involvement but simply don't have time to make the necessary connections. They would love to see their students' work publicly exhibited but worry, for example, that the essay on transgender experience Amy wrote might upset some of the parents. They face a daily balancing act between what would propel student engagement and what keeps the school out of the headlines. Often, when I read about what a school is doing, the lived reality is somewhat underwhelming. They want to open up their classrooms, but the gap between knowing and doing is just too great.

For this reason, when Ben and Adam asked me to write this afterword I needed to see if their talk was being walked.

The drive from the Atlanta airport to Tri-County Early College High School is full of cultural signals, some so glaring that it's hard to keep the car on the road. After you cross the state line between Georgia and North Carolina, every second billboard seems to be promoting gun ownership, gun sales, or (my favorite) a store specializing in "guns and drugs." As Homer Simpson said, "What could possibly go wrong?"

The appearance of Confederate flags is also quite striking. Mentally, I listed all the things I should avoid ("don't talk about politics, guns, religion, race, sexual identity, liberalism—anything really; just shut up!"). By the time I stopped at Haney's Family Restaurant in Murphy, North Carolina, I felt as though I'd walked into 1956. Coming from the industrial northeast of England, I was struggling to compute. How could a school from a Frank Capra movie be as cutting edge as they claimed? Where in this beautiful rural remoteness were they going to find all the adult mentors they claimed made the learning so authentic? And what the hell are "grits," anyway? I thought it was a synonym for resilience!

What followed could not have been more confounding than if you'd put me on a saddle and hit me with a banjo.

I spent the afternoon talking to TCEC students, who couldn't wait to show me their projects and talk with me about big, global issues. I've spoken to many students like these over the years. If you took away their Southern accents they could have been mistaken for kids in Queensland or Cornwall.

They were not blessed with privilege, but what struck me about these students was their ease around adults, their curiosity and articulateness, and their desire to do good in the world. For many of them, coming to Tri-County had been a culture shock. It was quite a leap to go from elementary and middle schools that made all their decisions for them and fed them a steady diet of test prep to splitting their time between taking classes at the partner community college and creating their own enterprises and projects at TCEC. But there was no doubt about what they were learning or where they were going next.

The biggest surprise was when I asked about the contrast between the experience of project-based learning (often derided as soft, "discovery learning") and the challenge of attending, and processing, a ton of tertiary-level lectures. "Oh, going to the community college is when we can ease up—sitting there, just taking notes is easy. It's way more challenging working on Mr. Owen's projects!" By the time I discovered that 75 percent of these students were graduating from twelfth grade with both a portfolio of socially purposeful projects and an associate degree, I was more than convinced—I was tremendously moved. Why, I kept thinking, do we put arbitrary limits on what we think kids can achieve? And if it can work here—in a region where teenage pregnancies, drug problems, and homelessness are rife—why doesn't everyone do it?

So, dear reader, trust me on this one: this school, this book, is the real deal. The lists of things you've read, that you can do as a teacher to open up learning, aren't some aspirational "wouldn't-it-be-nice" imagining. Every single item is achievable because they have used them all at Tri-County. And if they can make them work in disadvantaged rural America, in a school with precious few physical and financial resources, they can work anywhere.

It's often said that education does not always move in a linear forward motion. Instead, it swings like a pendulum, back and forth. For the past two decades we have lived through well-intentioned but ultimately doomed attempts to achieve equity through high-stakes accountability, cramming a so-called knowledge-rich curriculum into kids' heads and then relentlessly testing them. The effect has been, as the great John Holt once observed, like a gardener regularly pulling up plants to see how well the roots are progressing.

All around the world, however, the pendulum is swinging back toward knowledge and skills, theoretical understandings and learning by doing. Countries are recognizing that if students are to thrive in a volatile and uncertain future, they will need to be independent and agile learners. In the global auction for skills, Tri-County students will have a distinct advantage over students who have been taught only how to pass written tests.

But we need every student to benefit from the kind of experiences Ben and Adam describe in this book. That's where you come in. If you're a parent, give this book to your child's school leader and ask, "Why can't my child have this, too?" If you're a principal or teacher, have the courage to bring some of these approaches into your classrooms. The risks are low because, in truth, there's nothing in this book that the great education philosopher of the twentieth century, John Dewey, would have found unfamiliar. Dewey once famously said "education is not preparation for life; education is life itself."

And that's really all that this book is saying. The whole world is opening up—it's time for our learning to do the same.

David Price, OBE
Author of *Open: How We'll Work,
Live and Learn in the Future*

Appendix A

A Brief Overview of Open-Source Technology in Education

The Connexions Project at Rice University, founded in 1999 by Richard Baraniuk, was one of the first collections of digital educational materials made available free of charge. Now known as OpenStax CNX, it still operates under the philosophy that "scholarly and educational content should be shared, reused and recombined, interconnected and continually enriched." MIT followed in 2001 with the MIT OpenCourseWare project, which is considered the starting point for a worldwide movement to make academic content available for free to anyone.

From these beginnings, the open education resources (OER) movement has evolved to change the game in education, making high-quality teaching and learning resources available for free to students all over the world.[1] These resources have led to a significant improvement in one of the key equity issues facing public education: access to high-quality materials. Such value has been recognized within the philanthropic community, and now free OER are typically underwritten by significant investment from organizations such as the William and Flora Hewlett Foundation. Other OER are supported by crowdfunding, in which users donate what they feel is appropriate for the content they access and use.

Two highly popular OER platforms are Khan Academy and CK-12. The former is an extensive library of online YouTube lectures, tutorials, and support materials that allow teachers to "flip" their classrooms for core content and remediation. The latter provides an extensive database of educational materials that allow teachers to create and customize CK-12 Flexbooks, digital textbooks, and other content for their classes that are aligned to state and national curricular standards. Both of these and the exploding number of other OER platforms are helping level the playing field so that every school and teacher has access to high-quality education resources, assuming reasonable access to the Internet is available—a critical equity issue for sure.

Other platforms such as the Creative Commons (creativecommons.org) and OER Commons (oercommons.org) provide digital libraries with easy-to-understand terms of use that allow users to share, copy, curate, and repurpose a wealth of resources. Creative Commons specifically helps users legally share their work through the release of copyright licenses (known as Creative Commons licenses) that are free to the public rather than restricted for financial gain. Open-source content is typically free for everyone to use as they wish, as long as the work is attributed to the author.[2]

Other examples of open technology include blogs, online forums, wikis, e-books, open courseware, and various forms of social media. Some of the world's foremost universities have also made free courses available to the public with their massive open online courses (MOOCs). Harvard, Stanford, MIT, Duke, Princeton, University of California, Berkeley, and others have contributed to a growing body of free courses on everything from computer science to learning how to learn.

Even educators who are not familiar with the remixing characteristics of OER at least have experience with wikis, a tool that perfectly highlights how crowdsourced iteration is possible in an open-source context. Martin Weller, director of the OER Hub at the Open University in the UK (www.open.ac.uk) and author of several books on open education, describes the wiki as a web page that can be jointly edited by anyone. He recognized the potential power of wikis in the late 1990s as a technology that would open new, more collaborative interaction on the Internet and had the potential to democratize knowledge that used to be under the exclusive purview of academic elites.

Wikipedia was originally intended to solicit content from academic experts from across the world, but very few were interested in participating. After the initial concerns about quality faded away, Wikipedia took off and has now become one of the world's largest reference sites, operating completely in an open framework where anyone can edit and contribute content. Though at face value Wikipedia may be seen as an unreliable reference, at least one study has shown a 99.5 percent accuracy rate for its information.[3] Why? The crowd is a relentless quality-control mechanism. Compare the quality of Wikipedia to traditional science textbooks, which can become outdated astonishingly quickly, and you begin to see the power of open-source networks to create relevant educational resources.

There are two "must read" books for anyone who wishes to thoroughly understand how open education tools, resources, and knowledge can improve the quality of education. The first is the book *Opening Up Education: The Collective Advancement of Education through Open Technology, Open Content, and Open Knowledge*, edited by Toru Iiyoshi and M. S. Vijay Kumar and is freely accessible. This series of essays by recognized experts in the open education field describes examples of emerging innovations, as well as challenges that open education initiatives currently face. The second is the book *Open: The Philosophy and Practices that Are Revolutionizing Education and Science*, edited by Rajiv Jhangiani and Robert Biswas-Diener. It also provides a comprehensive description of how open-source resources affect pedagogy, teaching, and free access to data.

Finally, we found that the University of Pittsburgh Library was one of the best clearinghouses of OER and recommend it to anyone wishing to learn more about this topic.

Appendix B

A Portrait of an Open Way Learning Academy

Who wants to research this technology and bring their findings back to the team? What is needed to scale this work to other areas? What data are needed to better substantiate this solution? If you think this is a conversation at a Silicon Valley company, think again. These questions are routinely heard during the Critical Friends meetings at Tri-County Early College High School—biweekly meetings during which all teaching staff and administrators gather to collaborate, share ideas, and develop short-term and long-term actions to better meet the needs of their students. This is but one of the many reasons this small public school of choice situated in the rural mountains of Western North Carolina makes an ideal case study in the power of Open Way Learning.

This school, which you have probably never heard of, was modeled after schools you probably have heard of, including High Tech High in San Diego, California; the University Park Campus School in Worcester, Massachusetts; and Manor New Tech High School in Manor, Texas. With start-up support from the Bill and Melinda Gates Foundation, TCEC opened its doors in 2006 as part of the North Carolina New Schools Project and has a target population of first-generation college-goers, those at risk of dropping out, and other historically underserved populations.

Located on the campus of Tri-County Community College in Murphy, North Carolina, the high school has, from day one, had a motto of "doing school differently." That motto and the school's constant focus on looking more like a high-tech start-up and less like a traditional school has led it to embrace proven best practices such as competency-based education, project-based learning, place-based service learning, a biannual student-led e-portfolio review for parent teams, an emphasis on arts-integrated STEM, and one-to-one iPads. Its impressive track record on a variety of metrics lends solid credibility to the claim that its nontraditional approach works for its students and community.

One of the biggest honors for the school was being named a finalist (in the top fifty) in the XQ Super School Contest in 2015–2016. The XQ contest allowed the school to revisit and refine its vision, and although it did not win the XQ prize, those in the school's learning community committed to following through on their plan. Among other innovations, they implemented school-wide, cross-curricular, and cross-grade projects; flexible scheduling for students; formal outside experts or mentors for all project teams; and daily advisory time for students to reflect on and discuss social-emotional learning, postsecondary plans, Genius Hour, and academic goals. From a governance standpoint, TCEC implemented a business advisory council, formalized their classroom rounds, embedded teacher professional development, and became one of just over one hundred official Teacher-Powered Schools in the United States.

These elements of the school's approach to teaching and learning are all part of being an Open Way Learning Academy, one where collaboration is woven into the DNA of the school, where ideas are evaluated based on merit instead of the source, and where this free and open exchange of ideas leads to faster innovation to help each student find pathways for success. It's a place where on a daily basis students and staff openly share, collaborate, and create with people outside the school—among them local and global entrepreneurs, start-ups, nonprofits, and government. TCEC is a place where students innovate on existing initiatives and get their hands dirty working on things they care about. All of this helped TCEC be nominated in 2018 to become a member of the Global Schools Alliance, one of fifteen of the most highly innovative schools across the world.[1]

Does the school still have failures and face headwinds? Of course. But rather than engaging in the harmful bellyaching that often undermines organizational morale, those at the school bring issues to the forefront within a network of peers, in an environment of transparency and trust. That energy can then be focused on teaching excellence and can support a shared belief that no problem is too difficult to tackle. Sue Ledford, the school's founding principal, put it this way: "The level of trust among the entire school community has blossomed with this approach, producing confident thinkers and doers among the student population."

The school's success has come despite being relatively tiny, with an austere budget and small staff in a part of rural Appalachia facing significant economic challenges. This is ultimately what led us to tell this story, a story of how an Open Way Learning culture could be applied in any school, anywhere.

Notes

CHAPTER 1: WHAT IS OPEN WAY LEARNING?

1. "Scenes from the TCEC Hometown Heritage Project March 22nd 2018," YouTube video, 4:15, posted by Jason Chambers, March 26, 2018, https://www.youtube.com/watch?v=FdIIvjnf9QM.

2. Seth Godin, Twitter post, December 18, 2017, 2:04am, https://twitter.com/ThisIsSethsBlog/status/942697145483882496.

3. Gauri Sood, Shipra, and Rachna Soni, "Comparative Study: Proprietary Software vs. Open Source Software," *International Journal of Innovative Research in Computer and Communication Engineering* 4, no. 11 (November 2016), http://www.ijircce.com/upload/2016/november/8_Comparative.pdf.

4. Chris Burnett, "Open Source vs Closed Source—Which Is More Secure?" Franklin Fitch. June 13, 2017, http://www.franklinfitch.com/blog/2017/06/13/open-source-vs-closed-source-secure/.

5. "Red Hat Enterprise Linux," Red Hat, https://www.redhat.com/en/technologies/linux-platforms/enterprise-linux.

6. "List of Commercial Software with Available Source Code," Wikipedia, last modified April 15, 2018, https://en.wikipedia.org/wiki/List_of_commercial_software_with_available_source_code.

7. "Uncover the Building Blocks of the Universe," Higgs Hunters, https://www.higgshunters.org/.

8. "The Open Source Way," Opensource.com, https://opensource.com/open-source-way.

9. "OER Resources for Policy Makers," Council of Chief State School Officers, last modified February 16, 2018, http://www.ccsso.org/resource-library/oer-resources-policy-makers.

10. Charlie Reisinger, "Enabling Students in a Digital Age: Charlie Reisinger at TEDxLancaster," YouTube video, 15:29, posted by TEDx Talks, May 30, 2014, https://www.youtube.com/watch?v=f8Co37GO2Fc.

11. Katrina Stevens, "Twitter Exec Reports That Educators Dominate the Twitter-sphere," EdSurge, March 13, 2018, https://www.edsurge.com/news/2014-04-30-twitter-exec-reports-that-educators-dominate-the-twitter-sphere.

12. Aleszu Bajak, "Lectures Aren't Just Boring, They're Ineffective, Too, Study Finds," *Science*, May 12, 2014, http://www.sciencemag.org/news/2014/05/lectures-arent-just-boring-theyre-ineffective-too-study-finds.

13. "The Most Popular Talks of All Time," TED, https://www.ted.com/playlists/171/the_most_popular_talks_of_all.

14. "The Third Industrial Revolution," The Office of Jeremy Rifkin, https://www.foet.org/books/the-third-industrial-revolution/.

15. Bernard Marr, "Why Everyone Must Get Ready for the 4th Industrial Revolution," *Forbes*, April 5, 2016, https://www.forbes.com/sites/bernardmarr/2016/04/05/why-everyone-must-get-ready-for-4th-industrial-revolution/#63cbb9243f90.

16. Thomas Friedman, "While You Were Sleeping," *New York Times*, January 16, 2018, https://www.nytimes.com/2018/01/16/opinion/while-you-were-sleeping.html.

17. "New GenForward Poll on Technology: New Study Reveals Millennials Support for Net Neutrality, Concern over Technology Decreasing Available Jobs, and Experience Broadband Inequality by Race," GenForward, March 15, 2018, https://genforwardsurvey.com/assets/uploads/2018/03/GenForward-March-Technology-Report-Press-Release.pdf.

CHAPTER 2: PLANTING OPEN WAY LEARNING SEEDS

1. Jeffrey Mirel and Simona Goldin. "Alone in the Classroom: Why Teachers Are Too Isolated," *Atlantic*, April 17, 2012, https://www.theatlantic.com/national/archive/2012/04/alone-in-the-classroom-why-teachers-are-too-isolated/255976/.

2. Rob Asghar, "What Millennials Want in the Workplace (And Why You Should Start Giving It to Them)," *Forbes*, January 13, 2014, https://www.forbes.com/sites/robasghar/2014/01/13/what-millennials-want-in-the-workplace-and-why-you-should-start-giving-it-to-them/#60ec49ed4c40.

3. "Teacher Shortage Areas," U.S. Department of Education, August 29, 2017, https://www2.ed.gov/about/offices/list/ope/pol/tsa.html.

4. Karyn Dickerson, Taylor Milburn, Doyle Nicholson, Dave Orphal, Ben Owens, Sabrina Peacock, Joanna Schimizzi, and Nicole Smith, "Transforming Teachers' Careers and Compensation in North Carolina: A New Vision from Some of Our State's Best Teachers" (Center for Teaching Quality, August 2016), https://www.slideshare.net/educationnc/313823021-teacherleadershipandpay.

5. Dian Schaffhauser, "Race to the Top Funding Impact on Student Outcomes 'Not Clear,'" *The Journal*, November 10, 2016, https://thejournal.com/articles/2016/11/10/race-to-top-funding-impact-on-student-outcomes-not-clear.aspx.

6. Elaine Weiss, "Mismatches in Race to the Top Limit Educational Improvement," *Economic Policy Institute*, September 12, 2013, https://www.epi.org/publication/race-to-the-top-goals/.

7. "Six Sigma Tools," ASQ, http://asq.org/learn-about-quality/six-sigma/tools.html.

8. Pamela Spann, "The Negative Effects of High-Stakes Testing," paper written for Education Law and Policy 461, taught by Dean Kaufman, Loyola University Chicago, May 14, 2015, https://www.luc.edu/media/lucedu/law/centers/childlaw/childed/pdfs/2015studentpapers/Spann.pdf.

9. Sandra Christenson, Amy L. Reschly, and Cathy Wylie, eds., *Handbook of Research on Student Engagement* (New York: Springer, 2012).

10. David Conley and Linda Darling-Hammond, "Building Systems of Assessment for Deeper Learning," in *Beyond the Bubble Test*, by Linda Darling Hammond and Frank Adamson (San Francisco: Wiley, 2015), 277–310, doi:10.1002/9781119210863.ch10.

11. Martin Williams, "Is Competition between Schools Restricting Collaboration?" *Guardian*, October 31, 2016, https://www.theguardian.com/teacher-network/2016/oct/31/is-competition-between-schools-restricting-collaboration.

12. "Frequently Asked Questions," National School Reform Faculty, https://www.nsrfharmony.org/faq/; Deborah Bambino, "Critical Friends," *Educational Leadership* 59, no. 6 (March 2002), http://www.ascd.org/publications/educational-leadership/mar02/vol59/num06/Critical-Friends.aspx.

13. Clea Fernandez, Joanna Cannon, and Sonal Chokshi, "Japan Lesson Study Collaboration Reveals Critical Lenses for Examining Practice," *Teaching and Teacher Education* 19 (2003): 171–185.

14. Dick Startz, "Teacher Pay around the World," Brookings, June 20, 2016, https://www.brookings.edu/blog/brown-center-chalkboard/2016/06/20/teacher-pay-around-the-world/.

15. "XQ: Rethink," YouTube video, 4:18, posted by XQ America, September 18, 2017, https://www.youtube.com/watch?v=0asK-jjLPOo.

16. Thomas Skrtic, "The Special Education Paradox: Equity as the Way to Excellence," *Harvard Educational Review* 61, no. 2 (1991): 148–207, http://hepgjournals.org/doi/abs/10.17763/haer.61.2.0q702751580h0617?code=hepg-site.

17. Ellen Bacon and Lisa Bloom, "Listening to Student Voices: How Student Advisory Boards Can Help," *Teaching Exceptional Children* 32, no. 6 (2000): 38–43.

18. Adam Haigler, "Open-Source Learning in Action," Edutopia, June 9, 2017, https://www.edutopia.org/blog/open-source-learning-adam-haigler.

CHAPTER 3: CONSTANT COLLABORATION

1. Rob Kaplin, "America Has to Close the Workforce Skills Gap," *Bloomberg*, April 12, 2017, https://www.bloomberg.com/view/articles/2017–04–12/america-has-to-close-the-workforce-skills-gap.

2. "Talk: Great Man Theory," Wikipedia, May 10, 2018, https://en.wikipedia.org/wiki/Talk:Great_man_theory.

3. Linda Lambert, "How to Build Leadership Capacity," *Educational Leadership* 55, no. 7 (1998): 17–19, https://eric.ed.gov/?id=EJ563894.

4. Seymour Sarason, Murray Levine, Ira Goldenberg, Dennis Cherlin, and Edward Bennett, *Psychology in Community Settings: Clinical, Educational, Vocational, Social Aspects* (New York: John Wiley, 1966).

5. Dan Lortie, *Schoolteacher: A Sociological Study* (Chicago: University of Chicago Press, 1975), 195–97.

6. Carrie R. Leana, "The Missing Link in School Reform," *Stanford Social Innovation Review*, Fall 2011, https://ssir.org/articles/entry/the_missing_link_in_school_reform.

7. TNTP, *The Mirage: Confronting the Hard Truth about Our Quest for Teacher Development*, August 4, 2015, https://tntp.org/publications/view/the-mirage-confronting-the-truth-about-our-quest-for-teacher-development.

8. Bill and Melinda Gates Foundation, *Teachers Know Best: Teachers' Views on Professional Development*, 2015, http://k12education.gatesfoundation.org/resource/teachers-know-best-teachers-views-on-professional-development/.

9. "MetLife Survey of the American Teacher," MetLife, series of reports, https://www.metlife.com/about/corporate-responsibility/metlife-foundation/reports-and-research/survey-american-teacher.html.

10. David Rutkowski, Leslie Rutkowski, Julie Bélanger, Steffen Knoll, Kristen Weatherby, and Ellen Prusinski, *Teaching and Learning International Survey, TALIS 2013: Conceptual Framework* (Organisation for Economic Co-operation and Development, 2013), http://www.oecd.org/education/school/TALIS%20Conceptual%20Framework_FINAL.pdf.

11. Susan Kardos and Susan Johnson, "On Their Own and Presumed Expert: New Teachers' Experience with Their Colleagues," *Teachers College Record* 109, no. 9 (2007): 2083–2106, https://eric.ed.gov/?id=EJ820488.

12. James Klein and Doris Pridemore, "Effects of Cooperative Learning and Need for Affiliation on Performance, Time on Task, and Satisfaction," *Educational Technology Research and Development* 40 (1992): 39–47.

13. "Collaborative Learning: Group Work," Cornell University, Center for Teaching Innovation, https://www.cte.cornell.edu/teaching-ideas/engaging-students/collaborative-learning.html#impact.

14. Shirly Hord and William Sommers, *Leading Professional Learning Communities: Voices From Research and Practice* (Thousand Oaks, CA: Corwin, 2008), 113–15.

15. Judith Warren Little and Milbrey McLaughlin, eds., *Teachers' Work: Individuals, Colleagues, and Contexts* (New York: Teachers College Press, 1993), https://crceducation.stanford.edu/sites/default/files/teachers-work-1993_0_0.pdf.

16. Kaylan Connally and Melissa Tooley, *Beyond Ratings: Re-envisioning State Teacher Evaluation Systems as Tools for Professional Growth* (New America, March 2016), https://www.newamerica.org/education-policy/policy-papers/beyond-ratings/.

17. David Garvin, Amy Edmondson, and Francesca Gino, "Is Yours a Learning Organization?," *Harvard Business Review*, March 2008, https://hbr.org/2008/03/is-yours-a-learning-organization.

18. Robert Kaplinsky, "#ObserveMe," Robert Kaplinsky blog, August 15, 2016, https://robertkaplinsky.com/observeme/.

19. "The Opportunity Culture Principles—Home," Extending the Reach of Excellent Teachers Opportunity Culture, June 14, 2018, accessed July 29, 2018, http://opportunityculture.org/the-opportunity-culture-principles/.

20. Ben Owens and David Strahan, "Expanding Excellence: Teachers Cross District Lines to Learn with Peers," *Journal of Staff Development* 37, no. 3 (June 2016): 21–24.

21. Linda Lambert, "Beyond Instructional Leadership," *Educational Leadership* 59, no. 8 (2002): 37–40.

22. Richard Elmore, "Building a New Structure for School Leadership," *Shanker Institute*, Winter 2000, http://www.shankerinstitute.org/sites/shanker/files/building.pdf.

23. "Where Businesses Thrive," WeWork, https://www.wework.com/.

24. Amy Junge and Kim Farris-Berg, "15 Areas of Autonomy Secured by Teams of Teachers Designing and Running Teacher-Powered Schools," *Teacher Powered Schools*, July 2015, https://www.teacherpowered.org/files/Teacher-Powered-Autonomies-Detailed.pdf.

25. Helen Marks and Susan Printy, "Principal Leadership and School Performance: An Integration of Transformational and Instructional Leadership," *Educational Administration Quarterly* 39, no. 3 (2003): 370–97.

CHAPTER 4: FREE THE KNOWLEDGE

1. Charlie Reisinger, *The Open Schoolhouse: Building a Technology Program to Transform Learning and Empower Students* (published by author, 2016).

2. Ben Owens, "How to Embrace the Student Engagement Challenge," *Education Week*, February 28, 2018, https://www.edweek.org/tm/articles/2017/01/24/how-to-embrace-the-student-engagement-challenge.html.

3. "Project Oriented Learning," YouTube video, 3:59, posted by Jeff Robin, February 26, 2013, https://www.youtube.com/watch?v=ZTr3XfvrL3Y.

4. Matthew Harris, "The Challenges of Implementing Project-Based Learning in Middle Schools" (PhD diss., University of Pittsburgh, 2014), 91.

5. Information about the Buck Institute for Education is available at bie.org.

6. Gerry Everding, "Students Learn More If They'll Need to Teach Others," Futurity, August 12, 2014, https://www.futurity.org/learning-students-teaching-741342/.

7. Robert Wubbolding, "Glasser Quality School," *Group Dynamics: Theory, Research, and Practice* 11, no. 4 (2007): 253–61.

8. "This Is Doable—and Needs Doing," Mastery Transcript Consortium, http://mastery.org/this-is-doable-and-needs-doing/.

CHAPTER 5: INTREPID INNOVATION

1. Csikszentmihalyi, Mihaly. *FLOW: Studies of Enjoyment*. Chicago: University of Chicago, 1974.

2. Tom Vander Ark, "The High School Challenge: Improvement vs. Innovation," *Education Week*, April 24, 2013, http://blogs.edweek.org/edweek/on_innovation/2013/04/the_high_school_challenge_improvement_vs_innovation.html.

3. Terry Heick, "12 Barriers to Innovation in Education," TeachThought, August 29, 2017, https://www.teachthought.com/the-future-of-learning/12-barriers-innovation-education/.

4. "Jaguar Cage," Tri-County Early College, 2017, https://www.tricountyearlycollege.org/jaguarcage.

5. Alison Reynolds and David Lewis, "The Two Traits of the Best Problem-Solving Teams," *Harvard Business Review*, April 24, 2018, https://hbr.org/2018/04/the-two-traits-of-the-best-problem-solving-teams.

6. Adele Peters, "It's a Time for Disobedience: MIT Media Lab Will Pay $250,000 to Support It," *Fast Company*, March 30, 2017, https://www.fastcompany.com/3069027/its-a-time-for-disobedience-mit-media-lab-will-pay-250000-to-support-it.

7. Ellen Langer, *Mindfulness* (Reading, MA: Addison-Wesley, 1989), 136.

8. Karen Shakman, Jessica Bailey, and Nicole Breslow, "A Primer for Continuous Improvement in Schools and Districts," *Education Development Center*, February 2017.

9. Dale Frost, "How New Hampshire Transformed to a Competency-Based System," iNACOL, May 10, 2016, https://www.inacol.org/news/how-new-hampshire-transformed-to-a-competency-based-system/.

10. "Competency-Based Learning or Personalized Learning," U.S. Department of Education, https://www.ed.gov/oii-news/competency-based-learning-or-personalized-learning.

11. Mason Carpenter, Talya Bauer, and Berrin Erdogan, "Designing a High-Performance Work System," in *Management Principles* (December 29, 2012), section 16.5, https://2012books.lardbucket.org/books/management-principles-v1.0/s20-05-designing-a-high-performance-w.html.

CHAPTER 6: THE OPEN WAY LEARNING ACADEMY

1. David Leonhardt, "Schools That Work," *New York Times*, November 4, 2016, https://www.nytimes.com/2016/11/06/opinion/sunday/schools-that-work.html?_r=2.

2. Robert J. Marzano, "A Theory-Based Meta-Analysis of Research on Instruction" (Aurora, CO: Mid-Continent Regional Education Lab, 1998), https://eric.ed.gov/?id=ED427087.

3. John Hattie, *Visible Learning: A Synthesis of Over 800 Meta-analyses Relating to Achievement* (London: Routledge, 2008).

CHAPTER 7: BE THE SPARK

1. Robert Kegan and Lisa Laskow Lahey, *Immunity to Change: How to Overcome It and Unlock the Potential in Yourself and Your Organization* (Cambridge, MA: Harvard Business School Publishing, 2009), 1–2.

2. Chip Heath and Dan Heath, *Switch: How to Change Things When Change Is Hard* (Waterville, ME: Thorndike, 2011).

3. Frederick Hess, *Cage-Busting Leadership* (Cambridge, MA: Harvard Education Press, 2013), 5–9.

4. Thomas S. Kuhn, *The Structure of Scientific Revolutions* (Chicago: University of Chicago Press, 1970), 10–14.

APPENDIX A: A BRIEF OVERVIEW OF OPEN SOURCE TECHNOLOGY IN EDUCATION

1. Center for Educational Research and Innovation, *Giving Knowledge for Free: The Emergence of Open Educational Resources* (OECD, 2007), doi:10 .1787/9789264032125-sum-en.

2. Audrey Watters, "10 Open Education Resources You May Not Know About (But Should)," KQED, May 5, 2011, https://www.kqed.org/mindshift/11301/10-open -education-resources-you-may-not-know-about-but-should.

3. Mihai Andrei, "Study Shows Wikipedia Accuracy Is 99.5%," ZME Science, January 18, 2016, https://www.zmescience.com/science/study-wikipedia-25092014/.

APPENDIX B: A PORTRAIT OF AN OPEN WAY LEARNING ACADEMY

1. Global Schools Alliance, Home page, http://www.globalschoolsalliance.org/.

About the Authors

Adam Haigler is a biology, environmental science, and digital storytelling teacher at Tri-County Early College High School. He has worked with more than fifteen educational organizations as an instructor, founder, consultant, and administrator. Having experienced a wide variety of educational approaches and organizational structures, Adam has seen what works—and what doesn't. His training was primarily in progressive education and evolutionary biology with a focus on animal behavior.

Adam has also been a founder and director of experiential education organizations and worked as an outdoor and international educator for many years before entering public education. He was a contributing author for *The Gap Year Advantage*, a book touting the benefits of high school graduates taking time off before college.

Adam holds a bachelor of arts in education and a bachelor of science in biology from the Evergreen State College. He serves as a Teacher-Powered Schools ambassador and has been recognized as an Outstanding Educator by the North Carolina Science Teachers Association. He lives in Brasstown, North Carolina, with his wife and two children.

Ben Owens spent a twenty-year engineering career in manufacturing and R & D after earning a degree in physics from North Georgia University and a degree in mechanical engineering from Georgia Tech. Over the course of his career he saw firsthand the significant need to improve education so that students have the skills to thrive in a global innovation economy. That formative experience led him to leave the corporate world, earn a master of arts in teaching from Marshall University, and become a public school teacher in the rural mountains of Western North Carolina.

Ben taught physics and math for eleven years at Tri-County Early College High School, where he was able to refine his teaching craft and lead the school's efforts to implement innovative systems for personalized, experiential learning; competency-based learning; and school-wide, cross-grade and cross-curricular project-based learning. His unique teaching experience allowed him to become a 2014 National Teacher Fellow for Hope Street Group, the 2016 North Carolina Science Technology and Mathematics Center's 9–16 Outstanding Educator, the 2017 Bridging the Gap Distinguished Teacher in STEM Education, a Center for Teaching Quality Virtual Community Organizer, and a member of the Teacher Advisory Council for the Bill and Melinda Gates Foundation.

Ben is now a freelance education consultant who travels all over the world helping other educators, schools, districts, and networks as they strive to reach new levels of teaching and learning excellence. He lives in a sustainable farming community in Western North Carolina with his wife, Hygie.